I HOPE THIS BLE...
YOU BOTH.

CHRIS MACKEY

RICH IN HEAVEN

WHAT MATTERS MOST IS MORE THAN MONEY

RICH IN HEAVEN

DEDICATION

*To the richest person I know
on this side of heaven.
Kerri—my good thing.*

CONTENTS

PROLOGUE

The streets have been talking. The message about this man Jesus has reached every place from the big city to the lush countryside, even to remote villages. Knowing where he could find Him, Rich tracked Him down. The moment he saw Jesus, he took off running. There was a hefty crowd lingering about, but Rich didn't care; he threw himself at His feet, begging Jesus, "What must I do to get this life you've been teaching about?"

"What must you DO to GET? *Do* to *get*?" Jesus reasoned aloud. "There is a system where doing means getting—what does The Law say? If you want to keep on living, don't murder anyone, don't sleep with someone else's wife, don't steal from them, lie about them, or cheat them. Respect your parents—"

"Okay, I get it," Rich said. He *didn't* get it. "But Jesus—" he started, then thought, *Body count: zero murders, check. Haven't taken anything that wasn't already mine, wives or property. Check, check. No one could prove I lied about them or cheated them ... parents could do worse. Check, check, check!*

Now Rich was confident. "Jesus, anyone who knows me can vouch for me that I've kept these my whole life."

A mild wave of chuckles ran through the crowd. It was apparent that this was Rich's first time meeting Jesus face to face. Those who had been following Him for some time and listening to Jesus teach knew what He meant when He started quoting from The Law.

He always taught that anger in the heart was the root of murder and that lust in the heart was the root of adultery. He would tell them The Law wasn't about the external, something to be kept; rather The Law was internal, to be owned in the heart. His followers also noticed the commandments He didn't mention: (#1) Yahweh is the only true God worthy of being worshipped, so (#2) don't let anything get in the way of your desire for Him, and (#3) don't treat your access to Him like a worthless utility. Therefore, the root of idolatry, even if only in the heart, was still idolatry.

The crowd looked on, passing judgment, but Jesus wanted to know more. What was this man's story? What was it like to walk a mile in his shoes? Those *were* some nice shoes. As a matter of fact, Rich's whole outfit was quite chic for the area.

Rich had already revealed his philosophy on life through the question he brought to Jesus: if you want to get something, you've got to do something. He must've done a lot of doing to get everything he'd gotten. But there wasn't enough he could do to earn the promises of God. If he wanted all The Law promised, he'd have to do it all.

Poor guy, Jesus thought. Very poor, indeed. This man believes riches are a measure of what you have, but the truth is, riches are a measure of what you need. On the surface, this man has everything he could ask for and everything he could work for. But here he is on his knees, empty of true life.

His heart broke for Rich. The fact that he had no earthly needs was keeping him from a rich relationship with God. Jesus could tell Rich was sincere, but heaven couldn't just be another rung on Rich's ladder to success. If He loved Rich at all, Jesus knew He'd have to burst his bubble.

"Here's what you gotta do," Jesus explained. "Get rid of everything that is getting in the way of your desperate need for God. In this case, your comfortable lifestyle—your money, your possessions—give it all to the needy and you'll be rich in heaven. After that, follow Me and I'll show you the way to true life."

The tension was thick. The crowd fell silent. Rich tried calculating in his head. But as the list of his possessions piled up, it outweighed the offer Jesus had put on the table. He left, dejected.

As he was walking away, Jesus seized the moment to teach a new lesson, using Rich as an illustrated sermon. "People like Rich who can live without Me in the present will also live without Me in the future. It's going to be hard for all those like him to see heaven. So hard, in fact, it would be easier to squeeze a camel through the end of a needle than to squeeze all of them into heaven."

"If they can't get into heaven, is there any hope for us?" someone among them dared to ask.

"Only with God," Jesus replied. "Otherwise, everything I've taught you about the Kingdom of Heaven is impossible to obtain."

Though Rich walked away, Jesus left the offer on the table.

Whatever happened to Rich? Well, he *did* keep on living and he is still trying to find an easier way to heaven. Today, he continues to enjoy a comfortable lifestyle where he can provide for himself and his family. Even in tough times, there may be things he wants, but his every need is always met.

The message about heaven has gained much popularity throughout the years. And Rich has also built a following of his own. Most people think they have heaven. But everybody wants to be Rich.

I am Rich.

You are Rich.

Based on Mark 10:17-31; Matthew 19:16-30

INTRODUCTION

"With every head bowed and every eye closed. No one looking around. I want you to think about your life, the good and the bad. If you were to die tonight, do you know without a shadow of a doubt that you'd get heaven? If you were to stand before God while a movie of your life was replayed, would He invite you to live with Him for an eternity in heaven or would you spend an eternity apart from Him in the fires of hell? I am going to pray a prayer. If you say, 'Pastor, I don't know where I would go. Could you include me in that prayer?' I want you to raise your hand. With every head bowed. With every eye closed. No one looking around. We'll say a quick prayer and *then* we can go outside and play kickball. Go ahead, raise your hand."

I heard something about kickball. *It was Kickball Week!* My head was bowed but my eyes were barely closed. I could see most hands in the room were up. I put mine up as well in solidarity, showing the pastor that his job was done and we were all ready. (Ready for kickball.) That was my first time making "the decision" to be saved. I was eight years old that summer.

STEP ONE

If you're anything like me, you're reading this wondering what in the world you've gotten yourself into. Don't worry, this is a first for me, too. Buckle up! We're going on a journey. My name is Chris Mackey—*Hi, Chris Mackey*—and if I had to describe myself, I'd say I'm about as average as it gets. What this means is that, financially, I'm not qualified to teach you how to get rich and, spiritually, I'm not qualified to teach you about the path to heaven. I do, however, believe I'm uniquely qualified to teach you how to be rich in heaven.

Allow me to give you my credentials.

My Kickball Week salvation was a sham, but I knew I was saved well before that moment. My family had gone to church every Sunday since I was born, and every time the offering plate came by, my parents would always give my brother and me each a one dollar bill to drop in. They were training us up and raising us right; raising us Christian.

You couldn't tell me I wasn't a Christian. If you had skills, the best you could do was what that pastor did—make me question my ticket to heaven or convince me that my "Get Out of Hell Free" card had been burned up by the hellish things I had done that week. A distorted view on heaven, yes, but not an uncommon one. Throughout the years, in various circles, I heard those messages dozens of times, and each time the bark lost some of its bite. Apart from the imminent fear of hellfire or the eminent expectation of Kickball Week, was there any reason a kid like me would desire heaven, something so far away?

At the same time, a rival kingdom was winning my favor. Through music, movies, and TV, I was being taught a different plan where I didn't have to wait until I died to experience bliss. I still remember learning "the key to life" in 1998: "Money, Power, Respect". This rap song told me the first step was to get money; with that I could afford some power, and through power, finally earn others' respect. A distorted view of riches, yes, but not an uncommon one. It made so much sense. My parents were always breaking the bad news to me, saying why I couldn't have what I wanted, and every time the reason was the same— money. With this *key to life*, I cashed in my already cheap faith and placed it in the Bank of the American Dream. Step one: get money.

I got my first taste of money at age sixteen when I was hired as a sandwich artist at Quiznos Sub. Finally, I could have all of the things I was told we couldn't afford. I turned hard-earned money into fine upgrades to my car, like the DVD player with a touchscreen panel, the XBOX that I never played, the cheetah-print upholstery, and the rims with spinning hubcaps. Yes, I said spinning *hubcaps*. And any time I travel down the Loop 101 Freeway, I still keep an eye out for the one that got away during my trip to Desert Ridge Mall back in '04. Needless to say, the money went *fast*. I was living with my parents, with minimal responsibilities, so the majority of my paycheck was disposable income. What a fitting term—disposable. I couldn't find quick enough ways to get my money into the landfill. Oh, but I tried.

I discovered the quickest way to turn my paycheck into waste, physiologically speaking, was through my digestive tract. That's a poetic way of saying I spent most of my money on food. (Great, it's not even the first chapter and we're talking about poop.) When I made more money than I could eat, I spent the excess on the latest gadgets. I thought I had a passion for electronics—really, I just loved the feeling that I got when someone drooled over the colorful screen on my new mobile phone. (C'mon, we're talking the early 2000s.) Naturally, my toys became more and more expensive, so it became necessary to sell the months-old ones that now bored me. Before I even realized it, at seventeen, my side hustle had turned into a full-fledged business.

As luck would have it, I actually turned eighteen while working for a major credit card company. What better birthday gift could I receive as an employee than my very own bondage (pronounced: credit card) with a low interest rate? Now, with three sources of funding, I was eager to get to *Power* and *Respect*; why not get into the music business? So I launched a record label to support my friends' aspirations in hip-hop. First, we were recording songs, then we were booking shows, and then we released our music on CD and online for exactly what it was worth (that is, we gave it away for free).

Then came the cell-phone chargeback which will live in infamy. My PayPal account was randomly frozen, not allowing any activity to or from the account. At the same time, someone requested a $1200 refund because they didn't like the color of their phone. I promptly sent them a refund from my own bank. Once my PayPal account was unfrozen, they received a second refund. (Gulp.) The following week, an album-release party went awry, for which I was charged damages by a hotel. My account was overdrawn. Then came the fees. Is there anything more sadistic than charging someone for being broke? Back to step one. My electronics business was on the rocks and my record label was hemorrhaging cash quicker than I could find it.

A $1,500 credit limit goes fast.

So did the $3,000 and the $5,000 limit.

Three credit cards later, I was working at Guitar Center, enjoying the employee discount. If it were legal, I probably would have opted out of receiving a paycheck altogether and just left with the gear. In a matter of years, I had amassed a treasury of recording and DJ equipment. In a matter of weeks, everything was stolen from my new home, leaving behind nothing but debt and regret.

I've been on step one for over twenty years now. I could go on but I've got a whole book to bore you with the details. Let's just say my plan didn't work as I'd hoped. When the storms of life hit, I had nothing to show for all of the debt I was in. Whether it be time or money, I could easily think, *What a waste!* Today, I know the truth: none of these experiences were a waste to me.

As a college dropout, these experiences became my professors teaching me valuable lessons through the course of life. For instance, in the record label I started, I gained some useful business wisdom, from planning to execution. When my artists needed to record their music, I became a recording, mixing, and mastering engineer. When they needed an album cover, I taught myself graphic design. When no one was interested in listening to the music, I got into marketing, promotions, and web design. When they booked a show and needed a DJ, I figured that out, too. These are all skills that I still use today in my career and as a freelancer.

By far, the most valuable thing I've learned throughout my financial journey is that my way sucks. The three-step "money, power, respect" aerobics were exhausting. And my own efforts to achieve prosperity also proved fruitless. I swapped jobs, trades, industries, and businesses, hoping to remedy my issue. Like taking Tylenol for a tumor, I wasn't sure if I was helping or hurting myself in the long run. All these things lay perpetually on the surface, showing symptoms of the true sickness within me.

My way sucks. I'm *the common denominator*. I'm *the problem*.

LIFE AND DEATH

My financial story parallels my coming to the faith. I figured I was a decent Christian because I went to church every week and paid a tithe. But I found out just how shallow my faith was once my business took a dive. I couldn't wait until heaven to start living, but living life "my way" wasn't living at all. When I started my company, I named it KOH—Keep On Hustlin'—to remind myself and those I worked with to "never give up." So, it's no surprise that I ignored the urgent memos, taking far too long to face the facts—it was time to give up. My identity, my dreams, and my pride would suffer a nice blow as in one sigh, I went from entrepreneur to ordinary. My business had breathed its last. My faith was dead, too.

Getting acquainted with death was exactly what I needed. It was the qualifier to becoming rich in heaven. To be clear, giving up didn't qualify me to *write* this book; rather, it qualified me to *read* this book. Giving up was simply the moment I acknowledged I needed something that could transform my heart. A new way—most certainly not another "my way."

External physical force can change your direction, but no amount will change your heart. Persuasive arguments can change your mind, but none can change your heart. In my experience, there are only two things that affect the heart: life and death. That's the way I describe the positive and negative circumstances that compel us to reject the status quo and forego our natural desires in favor of what we truly need.

I want to tell you Gary's story. Like most of my fellow Guitar Center coworkers, Gary was a typical working musician. As such, he enjoyed nightly drinking and partying, was certainly a ladies' man, and he often lacked a filter. (Makes sense why we connected so well.) I recall one particular night when Gary pulled me aside at the end of our shift and told me his girlfriend was pregnant. Then, we shared an awkward silence while I attempted to discern whether he felt positively or negatively about the news. He cracked a faint smile and I could tell he was elated. I hugged him as I shouted, "That's awesome!" Gary was going to be a dad.

I witnessed something in the following months that I had never seen before. At the news of this new life, Gary's life began to dramatically change. See, Gary grew up struggling with his weight. Well, it wasn't really much of a struggle; regardless of what it was up against, love for food won. Food was heaven. Gary lived to eat. Any time he would indulge in the satisfaction of his palate, his delight in life would increase. From the outside, it would seem that these two elements went hand in hand, and those who live to eat will understand—the more, the merrier.

What Gary refused to admit was that the food he loved so much could be the death of him. His cholesterol was through the roof and he was at risk for a heart attack. Heart attacks run in Gary's family, affecting all of his uncles and his grandfather—they all survived them, but perhaps he wouldn't be so lucky. Gary was on the verge of becoming another statistic; his love for food was at odds with his love for life. If he wanted to continue to enjoy one, it would mean he would enjoy less of the other. He ignored that fact until a greater one dawned on him.

Gary was about to become responsible for the life of another human being. And the effects were night and day. Two major transformations began happening at once, right before my eyes.

First, we stopped going to lunch together; we stopped talking about our love for delicious cuisine, in fact, all we ever talked about was this new health kick he was on. What happened to his love for food? What the heck had gotten into him? What was *wrong* with him? Despite my constant antagonizing, Gary continued unfazed, even building momentum. He was getting results, too. Eventually, he reached his goal weight, losing almost 100 pounds. I had never seen anything like it, and he made it look easy.

When I asked him, his response was on par. It *was* easy. Gary decided that he would be around to see, love, and raise his daughter; that he wouldn't be a statistic in his family; that he would enjoy life beyond his belly. Some foods he could enjoy in moderation, others were considered poison, and every meal was an opportunity to affirm or abandon his position. He faced life and death daily, and each day he chose life.

The second transformation in Gary was internal. As if he could hear a forty-week clock ticking down, he sprang into action. Kids cost money. Drinking and partying was out. His complacent work ethic was behind him. He sold like crazy, rose through the ranks, and leaped from the manager of his department to the manager of the sales floor.

Gary was dozens of pounds lighter, but that's about the only thing that had changed externally. Something inside him birthed ambitions which brought him several pay raises and a move from commission to salary. In his preparation to become a father, Gary's priorities shifted. He never would have made these changes for himself, but now, his desire was to be a good dad. His new priorities favored this new life.

Life happens. At face value, you would think that phrase means something positive. Instead, we use the word "life" as a euphemism for the most troubling experiences we come up against. Still, we fight for life, celebrate life, and come to life, in the most triumphant fashion. And we say someone is "truly living" when he discovers his purpose.

Death happens. (That's not a real saying; I just felt like it was the best way to transition.) Death is certain. Death is such a dreadful subject, it's the one word we avoid using when someone actually—dies. However, we don't just attribute death to those who have passed away. We label dead anything of value that comes to an end. From relationships to music to laptop computers, they all end up in the same bin once their usefulness expires—dead.

Like Gary, we transform when we witness life and death situations. They penetrate our core with such intensity that we're forced to respond with an upgraded finesse. Whether you face a "life" experience, a "death" experience, or a "life-and-death" experience, every new experience requires a new level of growth within you. On the other side of these trials, a newer you awaits with a greater capacity and fewer needs. It all starts with life or death. When you begin to truly live, your heart will change, and when you begin to truly die, your heart will change.

YOUR TURN

So, what's your story? Maybe something has died in your life, or maybe you've found something worth living for. Perhaps you're in the middle of both like I was. If you will accept the challenge and look ahead, you will see the prize is very rich, and it's within reach. I wish there was a formula I could give you, but there isn't. Instead, I want to invite you to walk through the same transformational process that I did when I arrived at an impasse in my faith.

I'm not going to try to change your heart. That's not my job. But in the coming chapters, we will look at our priorities, resources, and experiences and weigh them against our convictions, Scripture, and the life of Jesus.

I've gotten to know many believers over the years and have found that a lot of our stories follow a similar pattern. It goes like this:

I was going my own way, which seemed right to me. Jesus loved me enough to rescue me at just the right time before my sickness could completely destroy me. He gave me a new heart that will last forever, complete with new desires. And now I live each day receiving from His Holy Spirit the strength I need to outwardly express what has happened inwardly. I am no longer interested in my own will, led by my wicked heart, but I long to see His will done on earth as it is in heaven. Day by day, I will look more like the one I remain closest to, so I choose to remain in Christ until He returns or calls me home.

I have found that trusting in Christ is the grand intersection of both a life and a death experience. No, this is not a story of how I came to faith and then God made everything better in my life. It didn't work that way for me. In fact, it was more like the opposite. It cost me everything. The only heaven on earth I knew was found in the respect of my friends and the work I did, so believe me when I say that leaving it all behind felt like hell. And somehow, this was *good news*. It was good news because in losing my life, I gained His.

God didn't have to do it this way. He didn't have to allow me a second or a third or a seventy-seventh chance. He didn't have to include me at all. But He did. In doing so, I learned the truth about riches and the truth about heaven. And this wasn't some hidden truth; it was right there in His Word. Jesus is King—today! Not just in the future, but right now. *That is the Good News.*

Jesus came preaching that heaven is more than a distant idea in the recesses of our minds but a powerful kingdom that is within reach. Everyone whose life has been transformed by King Jesus has been given the task of announcing the Kingdom of Heaven with their lives ever since. His message has to affect my message. This is at the center of everything I plan to outline in this book. Jesus didn't go to the cross in vain. Thus, everything in my life, and every part of my story is important to God. And in His great wisdom, He allowed my story to intertwine with countless other stories like mine.

I wrote this book for me—a full-blown financial and spiritual mess amid recovery. Keep that in mind if you read something that offends you. My hope is that as I reveal some of the challenges in my journey, you will begin to challenge yourself in your own walk with Christ. If I hit my goal, you will learn what God says about money, you will discover the source of all provision, you will be able to rightly understand what importance finances should have in your life, and you will learn how to best manage what you've been given.

While I didn't write this to be a workbook, I will ask you questions from time to time. I encourage you to document your journey and write down any of the questions or answers that resonate with you. Invest in a small notebook to complete the exercises mentioned. You will find great wealth in being able to see how far you've come and remembering what God was saying throughout. (You will also find great wealth puns; they are all intended. You're welcome.)

This content has been prayerfully examined and tested by yours truly. It really relieves the pressure to know that I'm my own first customer and I'm writing to myself. I pray that you will be richly blessed beyond measure from applying the biblical principles in this book. I pray that the eyes of your understanding will be enlightened and you will receive exactly what you need to bring heaven into this season of your life. Most of all, I pray that you will see Jesus in a new way and be inspired to a richer relationship with Him.

GOOD NEWS SANDWICH

Have you heard the term "compliment sandwich," where criticism is given in the haze of two glowing positives? It's often used in the arts and business communities to communicate negative information to someone while minimizing their misery. I take one issue with a compliment sandwich: no good sandwich has ever been named by its bread—yes, I'm even including the bagel burger and the croissant breakfast sandwiches.

A true sandwich should be named by what's in the middle. So when I tell you that I've got a good news sandwich for you, trust me, it's aptly named. In this good news sandwich, the good news is in the middle.

Bad news: This probably isn't the book you were expecting to read. It wasn't the book I was expecting to *write*. It won't answer all of your financial questions or dive into your personal portfolio. Maybe I'll write that book one day in the future. If you're reading this from the future, I apologize from the past in advance.

Good news: If you are looking for a biblical approach to finances, this is probably the book you need to read first. In light of the Good News of Jesus, you will better understand what the Bible has to say on the subject of money.

Bad news: It likely doesn't say what you want it to say or what you think it says or even what your church of choice may teach. You will come to learn that the truth is a far more challenging standard. But that's not the bad news; the truth is never bad news. The bad news is that once you get this information, you'll be responsible for how you respond to it.

Bon appétit!

1

THE MOST IMPORTANT QUESTION

What is most important?

Have you ever in honest contemplation felt the need to ask the question, "Can rich people get into heaven?" If you are reading this book, I'm assuming you grew up in a predominantly Christian-influenced culture. If that is the case, you likely read that question and thought, "That's absurd. Anyone can get into heaven."

Case in point: there is that one Bible verse that everyone knows, Christians and non-Christians alike, and somehow we all know it in the King James Version. In John 3:16, we learn that heaven's promise of eternal life is for "whosoever believeth." Case closed.

I'm not at all looking to make a counter-argument. Jesus *is* indeed for everybody and anyone *can* have heaven if they want it. Jesus, who is quoted in John 3, however, is the same guy quoted in Mark 10 drawing a line in front of the rich and their possessions. It can be construed from the text, at the very least, that Jesus doesn't find that question absurd.

> "How hard it is for the rich to enter the Kingdom of God!" This amazed them. But Jesus said again, "Dear children, it is very hard to enter the Kingdom of God. In fact, it is easier for a camel to go through the eye of a needle than for a rich person to enter the Kingdom of God!"   (Mark 10:23-25)

Note to self: never make Jesus repeat Himself. The second and third time around, His point went from "hard to enter" to "very hard" to nearly impossible! If you read this and are thinking, *Good luck, rich folks*—you are rich folk. Even if you are in the bottom 5 percent socioeconomically in America, you are still more well-off than two-thirds of the rest of the world.[1] In the later chapters, we will discuss how you can choose whether you want to be needy or blessed simply by looking at what you have differently, but like it or not, you are the rich. So anytime you read in the Bible something that addresses the rich, be sure to pay close attention. It might be talking about you. End sidenote.

Wait, can having riches disqualify me from life in paradise with Jesus or not? Don't I just need to believe in Him? In the Bible, the words *believe*, *faith*, and *trust* all share the same root in Greek. We tend to see these as separate things, but I prefer to use the word *trust* since, like the Greek, the noun and the verb are the same. It's not so much that the rich will have a hard time qualifying for access to heaven; Jesus demonstrates that those who are experiencing their own heaven now will find it difficult to want the real thing when it comes if it means putting their trust in something other than their riches.

This was also a culture where the rich all benefited from a corrupt system that built its extravagant wealth on the backs of the less fortunate. To be rich was to be complicit in heartless disposition toward others. It's no surprise that Jesus would see a barrier between the oppressors and the Kingdom, considering the minority culture in which the Church was born.

Since then, what's changed? The tables have turned and Christianity is no longer the counter-cultural movement fighting opposition both from the world powers in authority and the religious majority. Today, the Church is both the religious majority and in the highest level of governing authority in many places. Yet the text of our Bibles remains, and we must consider how the words of Jesus in Mark 10—an indictment on the oppressive powers and the complicity of the religious majority—may now find us modern-day First World Christians in its crosshairs.

It's easy to read Jesus's words in context and assume all the rich people in His day were jerks. But now that the spotlight is on us, is there room for nuance? When Jesus started His ministry, many were astounded at His teachings, which began to draw large crowds wherever He went. The Sermon on the Mount, recorded in Matthew 5-7, gives us a glimpse into what Jesus was teaching on any given day to those who chose to follow Him. It starts with the Beatitudes, which acts as a table of contents for the discussion that follows. This is how He chose to start:

> "Blessed are the poor in spirit, for theirs is the kingdom of heaven."   (Matthew 5:3 ESV)

Heaven belongs to the poor in spirit. The NLT translates the phrase "poor in spirit" as "those who are poor and realize their need for him." I think this best illustrates the barrier between the rich and the Kingdom. It's not wanting heaven, it's needing it. Rick Warren says, "You never know God is all you need until God is all you have." It is the poor who are blessed enough to know this as a fact, while the rich have to believe it in theory. The rich have far more than just God. James understood the point Jesus was making and said this:

> Listen to me, dear brothers and sisters. Hasn't God chosen the poor in this world to be rich in faith? Aren't they the ones who will inherit the Kingdom he promised to those who love him?
> (James 2:5)

Our standard definitions of rich and poor are based on what you have. In this case, Jesus and James highlight what is possessed by the poor as opposed to the rich. Here's a shortcut for this book: Do you want to be rich in heaven? Become "poor in this world" and "rich in faith." This means emptying yourself of the need to be satisfied by what the world has to offer. This looks like telling the world "I've had enough!" and trusting God to meet your every need.

In the middle of Jesus's grand speech, we find another set of verses many of us know in the King James. In "The Lord's Prayer," Jesus gives His disciples a model for how to pray. I'd like to highlight two often-overlooked features. (See Matthew 6:9-13.) The first appears in the initial phrase "Our Father." Right off the bat, this is shown to be a corporate prayer shared with a community of equals. Jesus is teaching His followers what it means to be meek—regarding others as higher than ourselves (see Philippians 2:3). We ought to think about "us and ours" instead of "me and mines". And by addressing God as our Father, we are sharing an equal status as His children.

The second highlight is on the phrase "Give us today the food we need" (Matthew 6:11). We're so used to the saying "daily bread" that we most likely don't think about its meaning. This verse is asking Father God to look after our family of believers, ensuring they never miss a meal. There is an assumption here that if you are faithfully following Jesus, you will not always know where your next meal is going to come from.

For those who pray this prayer with a full fridge, we are forced to imagine what those words could mean for us. When we ask for today's "daily bread," we say it metaphorically to mean the strength to get through our workdays or the Bible verses to help us combat the most pressing issues we're facing. But this isn't an individual prayer; it's corporate. So we either must be living hand to mouth, or we need to pray as if the concerns of those belonging to a different status are in fact our own.

Jesus concludes this chapter by explaining why we shouldn't worry. Do you notice the things He assumes His followers would have to worry about? (See Matthew 6:25.) Food, drink, and clothing. Again, we read this portion of the sermon and pretend that Jesus is talking figuratively about the concerns of life, such as which field of study we should take in school or where we should buy our next home. But the context is clear: Jesus is talking about literal food. The Kingdom of Heaven belongs to those who would, under normal circumstances, worry whether they will "have enough food and drink, or enough clothes to wear."

For us, it's the exact opposite.

Have you ever opened your refrigerator or pantry and seen an endless array of *nothing to eat*? Or in your closet, swiping through hundreds of hangers only to find *nothing to wear*? This day and age is much different than what Jesus described. I know this is a broad generalization, but most followers of Christ aren't struggling with not having enough; they have too much junk in the trunk. (Take that how you wish.)

John 3:16 applies just as much today as it did when it was spoken. Whosoever trusts in the saving power of the Son can and will share in His eternal glory in heaven. Our biggest obstacle today is not what we lack, but the overabundance we have in everything. On this journey, we're going to take inventory of everything we have to our advantage and hold it up to the light of God. This book isn't so much concerned with whether or not we will get into heaven but whether the concerns of heaven will get into us.

DISORDER

I love making up words. Truth be told, I just like to start fights in the That's Not A Word yard and employ the Latin Root Mafia to back me up. I am eager to share some of my made-up words with you, and there's nothing a red underline can do to stop me. One of my great joys in life is admiring different languages and comparing words across translation. If you talk to me for an extended period of time, I can guarantee you that my brain will at some point resemble a spelling bee—repeating a word several times and sounding it out slowly before asking, "What is the language of origin?" I think a psychiatrist would call that ADD. Hmm ....

I actually found that out the hard way while participating in a church-wide Bible reading plan. Everyone was to fast, pray, exercise, and read the entire Bible in forty days. They gave us a postcard with the specified chapters to read for that day, and to my surprise, the reading took nearly two hours each day to complete. Juggling fasting, work, church, family, volunteering, and the many other obligations pressing for my attention proved to be an overwhelming challenge. Only a few days into it, I was ready to throw in the towel.

Then a friend told me about audio.

He explained to me that there was a website where the Bible is available for online listening. I thought, *That's a great idea! Why didn't I think of that?* It was a game-changer. Now anytime I had to sit in rush hour traffic or wait for a pot of water to boil, I could complete the daily reading. I was back on track and the challenge became a cinch. It was amazing.

I was listening to a dramatized version of the Bible, complete with music, background sound effects, unique voices for dialogue the whole nine. One day, I decided I would conduct an experiment. Surely, I could save time by skipping the hoopla and reading the chapters myself. I clicked Play and for the next eight minutes, I listened and followed along on my screen, even patiently tolerating the elaborate musical interlude at the end of the chapter. Phase one was complete, and now it was my turn. I checked the clock and began reading the same chapter again starting from the top. Fifteen minutes later, I became aware that I was no longer in the same neighborhood in which I started. I was on another tab searching the Hebrew lexicon for all the uses of the word "lost", only to see my own picture. I returned to where I left off—only two paragraphs in.

Oh, my gosh! I think I've got ADD.

Though I wasn't in a position to make a diagnosis, my experiment was conclusive: audio was my best bet for staying on task if I truly wanted to read anything. You must understand, I have always hated reading and I still do. But that's not because I'm indifferent to the results; I just abhor the method. I love receiving information. I love knowing the whole story. And thanks to the advancement of audiobooks and the Bible in audio formats, there are great solutions for the millions of people who are like me but still want to grow in their knowledge of God. And, yes, I completely understand the irony that I must read this book several times before it's published. Recording an audio version of this book is a top priority because otherwise, I might not read it again. I mean, if this book was already on audio, I never would've written it.

I write all of that to prepare you: I like to parse phrases, and sometimes I rationalize in the key of ADD. Even though it may appear as if I've taken a wrong turn at Albuquerque, trust me, I'm going somewhere. Like starting a fire, sometimes it's important to gather a bunch of materials in a wide range of sizes and then focus a spark onto the many minor pieces, which, once sustained, slowly rouses the bigger things.

SET A FIRE

As mind-blowing as the fire analogy was for you, I'm sure there are some who are saying, "Explain yourself, Chris." In almost everything we build, we start with a foundation, then we build our way up, beginning with the weightier matters and progressing to the minutiae for the finishing touches. But we're not building a house here. Often, when it comes to our understanding of heaven, just like our understanding of riches, our problem isn't a lack of experiential material; perhaps we have too much.

> We use God's mighty weapons, not worldly weapons, to knock down the strongholds of human reasoning and to destroy false arguments. We destroy every proud obstacle that keeps people from knowing God. We capture their rebellious thoughts and teach them to obey Christ.
> (2 Corinthians 10:4-5)

Paul was hearing some hollow criticism about him and his team coming from certain Corinthian Christians, and he was hoping to set them straight by appealing to them in a letter before he arrived in person. He likens their thought patterns and human reasoning to strongholds. There's nothing inherently wrong with a stronghold; it is a structure that's intentionally built to be a safe place. However, with effective strongholds, we tend to get comfortable in the safety of the structure more than we rely on God. This is how a place of safety can leave us vulnerable to the enemy's attack. Our place of strength becomes our weakness. Paul explains, if there's a belief system we are clinging to which keeps us from knowing God's truth, it's gotta come down.

The methodology we're using is gathering everything that we know and strategically arranging it—thoughts, beliefs, aspirations, words, actions, habits, and identity—and lighting the spark of God's Word onto it. If it ignites enough small areas of your life, the victories in those areas will function as kindling to set the larger matters ablaze.

There are a couple of drawbacks to this method. As quickly as a motivational thought can catch fire, inspiration is ephemeral. It fizzles out. In order for a log to catch fire, the kindling needs to heat it past its fire point—the temperature at which an object will stay aflame. It doesn't take a lot of sparks (God's Word) to ignite the areas we're going to address; that's the easy part. We even achieve brief victories with little effort. We run into two challenges with this kindling: it has to light and it has to last. If it doesn't light, we'll make quite an impression, but only for a moment. If it doesn't last, our efforts will be fruitless and before we start all over, we'll have a mess to clean up.

How do we ensure our victories will light? Give glory to God for them. Reaffirming your belief in what the Word of God says is like fanning the flame onto your winning streak. Getting into the rhythm of doing this is also how you can ensure the kindling will last. A winning streak brings with it momentum, yet we often lack the discipline necessary to sustain victories long enough to affect our character long-term. There's no simple fix for discipline, but we will address it in the later chapters.

The other drawback we face is the one I opened the chapter with: we are overexposed to a money-centric world, especially in the West, and our approach to finances is usually one derived from a variety of ideologies.

God forbid you resort to Google to remedy your dry mouth—you'll find you're either dehydrated or you could have a severe lifelong genetic abnormality. Unfortunately, the same phenomenon is present with financial advice. Financially speaking, we often treat our issues with a blood transfusion when a simple glass of water would do. And vice versa. The goal, then, is to sort out the myth from the fact, the vital from the dispensable, and the effective from the futile so that we know what we're working with.

> *Financially speaking, we often treat our issues with a blood transfusion when a simple glass of water would do.*

Our world is really not as different from the one Jesus lived in as we would like to think. Surely there were plenty of kind rich people in His day. But because they benefited from the same broken system that produced the grave injustices which exploited the poor, the sick, orphans, widows, and immigrants, Jesus didn't let any of them off the hook. Which side are we on today? We give preference to the wealthy because we assume if they are making a lot of money, they must be doing something right. When we do this, we perpetuate the notion that those at the top are above scrutiny. Now, because we also live in a Christianity-dominated world, we falsely attribute our audacity to Christ. Should His words excuse us now?

The first step in moving toward real solutions is recognizing the real problem. When it comes to finances, we figure the problem is obvious: you either don't make enough money or you spend too much of it. There are thousands of books, articles, apps, websites, and strategies built to address those shortfalls. Make no mistake, this is not one of those books. My goal isn't to find new solutions to the same old problem but to ask better questions. I want you to see something in God's Word that's always been there but which you haven't seen before.

It's easy to miss that which is happening around you all the time. Does a fish realize it's always wet? Have you noticed how nearly everything in life revolves around money, demands money, rewards with money, abuses money, represents money, or is related to money in some way? If so, you're either a really woke fish, or you've spent enough time out of water to appreciate it. As with most fish in the sea, however, many people will go their entire lives and never have to consider how they handle water or what it means to be aquatically stable.

A fire and a water analogy in the same chapter. Kudos.

If the average person can make it through life just fine without this information, then why does this even matter? That's a great question; I'm glad you asked. Firstly, you have this book—a book about what God has to say about money—so you're not average. If you're not sure how to take that statement, let's just call that a compliment. Secondly, when viewing statistics regarding debt, spending, and long-term wealth, it is clear that the average is *not* just fine.[2]

Now that we have wrecked the implications of the first half of the question, let's examine the second.

WHY?

I'm not very good at choosing favorites. But if I had to choose, *why* would be one of my favorite words. I first came to love the word when I took a Spanish class in high school. The Spanish word for *why* is *por qué*, which is actually two words literally meaning, "for what". When I learned this, it unlocked a whole new meaning of the word for me. I guess I never thought of what the word *why* meant; to me, it was just the beginning of a question and one of many similar-sounding interrogatives like *who, what, which, when,* and *where.*

I never considered that perhaps all of those words came from the same origin. I don't want to get too technical, so this explanation may be overly simplistic, but think of it as a fill-in-the-blank. These types of words suggest there is a piece of information missing. It's a way for us to make reference to the unknown. Once we've invoked one of these filler words, what was previously unknown becomes solid enough for us to look past the obscurity and discuss it further.

For example, we say *he* or *she* when we are talking about a person we know; yet, when the person is a mystery, we use *who*. In the same way, once we find out *when* something is going to happen, we call it *then*. On the show *Jeopardy*, the contestants are told to give their responses "in the form of a question." The form, however, changes with each response depending on the subject. Consider this: the questions, "Who is it?" "What is it?" and "Which is it?" are all basically the same question. The difference? The unknown is either a person (who), not a person (what), or a smaller part belonging to a larger set or series (which).

The children of Israel got what I'm saying. In Exodus 16, we see them ask that exact question when God miraculously sends them food. God declared that they would eat meat in the evening and bread in the morning. They were familiar with the meat—that was quail. Thank God for quail. And now for breakfast? "What is it?" God called it bread, but they had never seen bread like this before. They still ate it, but sadly never really figured out the answer to their question. They kept calling it "What is it?" (transliterated as *manna*) and the name stuck. (Spoiler alert: Jesus later answered their question in John 6.)

Whether or not my explanation makes any sense to you, it is amazing to think how much of this concept we actually grasp, since we regularly formulate sentences and use these words properly without even thinking. The main point that I gather is this: *why* will look different for everyone because we all have different *whats*.

And then there is *for*. I don't know that I am capable of making the word *for* seem as awesome as I did with *what*, but I'll give it a try because it truly is. *For* is a word that indicates purpose. It either helps explain the reasoning behind something or the motivation derived from that thing. Speaking of Christ's role in the vastness of creation, Paul pens, "Everything was created through him and for him" (Colossians 1:16). We can also use *for* to affirm our support of someone or something. My favorite example of this usage appears in Paul's letter to the Romans: "If God is for us, who can ever be against us?" (Romans 8:31).

Either way it's used, *for* assumes that we are talking about someone or something, which brings us back to *what*. *For what?* When we ask *why*, we are basically inquiring about the reason (*for*) in a thing (*what*). We are all involved with a plethora of *whats* each day. Every *what* has at least one *for* that it belongs to. These *fors*, both positive and negative, reveal certain elements of our character, like values and priorities.

Sometimes we are not aware of the reasons for what we do, and sometimes we don't recognize what something was for until after it has been removed from our lives. And then, there are moments like right now, when we get to assess the *whats* and *fors* of our lives in order to learn something about ourselves we could not have known otherwise. We stand to learn a lot about ourselves by asking this one question. The "most important" question is the question "what's most important?"

I have found that the best way to make this assessment is to make a list. In the following chapter, we will come up with our Why List so we know what we're working with. From there, we can discover what's most important. Everyone has a different starting point but we're headed to the same destination—rich in heaven. Your *why* will not be the same as my *why* and that's okay. Because we are all unique, our *whys* will be the reason the work that follows is worth it.

At this point, I totally understand the temptation for you to bookmark this page and set this book down until never. That's usually what I do when a book I'm reading recommends that I bust out pen and paper. After all, I'm usually listening to the book while working so it's not really an option. I'd like to stress the importance of having this list, yet I also wish to dissuade you from being overwhelmed. It's a lot like when your boss, knowing how busy you are, stops by your office to explain why you're the best person for some ad hoc extra work.

This is definitely a "Hey, whenever you get a chance ..." moment.

Feel free to read through the next chapter in its entirety

without worrying if the book will lose its charm when you don't participate. As we go along, the lessons will gradually become more practical and suggest you return to Chapter 2 in order to appropriately apply them.

Are you ready to find out what's most important?

2

CLOSING THE GAP

*Discouragement is the inflation
of your resistance, depreciating
the currency of your dreams.*

I could have made myself a Why List long before I started cleaning up my act. I was sucking up to my boss when he recommended I read a classic book, *The 10 Natural Laws of Successful Time and Life Management.* Not a chance! Instead, I bought it and just kept moving the bookmark every few days. (I reject your judgment.) Four years later, after I learned about audiobooks, I gave it a whirl. In it, author Hyrum W. Smith challenges the reader with two questions:

- What are the highest priorities in my life?
- Of these priorities, which do I value the most?[3]

The result of these questions should form what Smith calls your "governing values"—that is, the principles by which you choose to live and the standards by which you judge a thing as worth your effort to obtain it. When you ask yourself the first question, don't worry about the order; just focus on the things that are important to you and write them down. You'll want these items to describe the ideal you, but not the world's version of the ideal you. Here are some ways I rephrased the question to help myself discover my values:

- What do I want more than anything?
- What makes me feel most alive/gives me the most energy?
- What could I never have too much of?
- What do I want others to know about my life?
- What am I willing to die for?

Once you have a list of the values that matter to you most, do your best to prioritize that list. If your list is fairly long, I've found that breaking it into smaller groups makes it easier to manage. Try rating each item 1 through 5, with 1 being a top priority. Then, go back and rank all of the 1's, 2's, 3's and so on. You can now rewrite the list in order as one complete document, and to top it off, write a sentence that describes why each item means something to you. These are your *fors*.

After you've completed and reviewed your document, the fun begins. On a separate page, start jotting down things associated with each value. These are most likely going to be actions, but if not, spend a moment converting them. For example, if Creativity is one of your values and you wrote down "music" to support it, you could say "writing music," "singing a song," or "listening to music" instead. There will be some activities you already engage in and some you don't. There are no right or wrong answers with this, either. As long as the activities are ones you could do to display, solidify, or enjoy the area more fully, you are good to go.

(Okay, so I guess that means there *are* wrong answers, but just don't think too hard.) These are your *whats*.

If you're as odd as me, you may also want to try doing the same exercise in reverse. You'd do this by listing all the activities in which you participate on any given day; those will become your *whats*. Once you've made that list, go back and ask what's the point of doing those things. This can be one word or a phrase, but the goal is to make it as clear and succinct as possible. Once you have indicated the purpose you've found in an activity, write it down next to the item in a separate column. Those are the *fors*.

Similar to what we did in the first method, the next step is to take these statements of purpose and rank them on a separate piece of paper. Rankings are purely subjective, and you will find this exercise is most effective when you're being honest with yourself.

As you review your Why List, I'm sure, like me, you will find some discrepancies. Reading through the practical items on my list, I was confronted with disappointment and disbelief. I thought to myself: *This can't be all.* Then I took notice of my most aspirational virtues heckling me from the top of the list. Forget the bullseye—I'm not even hitting the dartboard. My thought was: *All this can't be.*

Talk about a discouraging exercise.

> *Discouragement comes when you rank your resistance above your motivation.*

I was discouraged because I was realizing that my present life did not match up with my ideal life. Of course, when we get into a ranking mindset, we immediately become critics. So this feeling of discouragement is just another ranking rising to the surface. Discouragement comes when you rank your resistance above your motivation. Hitting a roadblock at this point in the journey simply means that introspection and making lists isn't a bigger deal to you than peace and freedom. That's valuable information.

Whenever reality visits your expectations, there will be casualties. The greater the gap between your aspirations and reality, the greater your resistance will be. In the wake of reality, resistance is the somber scene of your heart as you bury those unmet expectations. If, like me, you're discouraged, it's because you're learning something new. This is actually a sign that the process is working so far. So keep going. Making a list is not the goal of this exercise; finding out what motivates you is.

Perhaps your personality doesn't object to tedium, or maybe you are just more motivated than I was. (If you enjoyed every bit of these exercises, I'd like to read your book on how to make the process more enjoyable—just make sure it's available in an audio format.)

The truth is, none of us are exactly where we'd like to be—living the way we believe is best. If we ever get there, we'll need to adjust again the following day since we as a people are continually changing. The pressure is not all internal, either. Meet a new person, start a new job, or drive past that new restaurant and you'll be faced with an all-new invitation to reprioritize your life. What I'm attempting to reiterate here is this: if it has not happened yet, there will come a point within the process of aligning your present lifestyle with your strongest ideals when you will be greeted with the opportunity to become discouraged.

Allow me to share the profit of my experience with you on this. In my first attempt at writing my list, I desperately wanted family to be somewhere near the top. I've always admired people who have a tight bond with their families and envied those who make the time to see and talk to their family members on a daily basis.

I was not living such a life. Sure, I didn't then nor do I now see my family as often as I'd like. But this gap between my hope and reality was Grand Canyon wide. As I explained before, that's sure to mean grand resistance.

I know I'm not the only one who's done this. Have you ever taken part in the Funeral Formalities? I'm not talking about delivering the eulogy. There's a funeral. You haven't seen the whole family come together since last Thanksgiving. It's been about ten months, and now at the funeral, you and another family member share this dialogue:

> "Hey, there! Long time no see."
> "Yes, it's good to see you. How have you been?"
> "I've been well, thank you for asking. How about you?"
> "Same here. How are the kids?"
> "Oh, they're great! Junior is about to start high school next week."
> "Wow, high school, already?! That's crazy, I can't believe it."
> "Yep."
> (AWKWARD SILENCE)
> "Well, it was good seeing you."
> "Yeah, it was good to see you, too."
> (HERE IT COMES)
> "We've got to get together more often."
> "Yes, definitely. And let's not wait until another funeral to do it."
> (END SCENE)

I'm not going to say that these Funeral Formalities are never the beginning of new family practices, I've just had to come to terms with the fact that my tank doesn't run on good intentions. I didn't aspire to be a family man who holds getaways and reunions all the time. The word "reunion" even made me a little sick to my stomach. I just liked the idea of people in my family *seeing* me that way. But as much as I tried to lie to myself, I couldn't bring myself to schedule any actions to improve that area—even when I had the time.

This is my first piece of advice when it comes to dealing with the resistance gap: stop lying to yourself. You need to adjust your values to be realistic. Honesty is key. If you don't really value something, be honest with yourself and don't put it to the top of your list.

My second piece of advice is for you to adjust your life to your values. Once you've thought this through and are confident this list faithfully represents your highest virtues, then it's time to own any discrepancies. This should provide a new lens through which you can view the things you do. Allow me to share once more.

Being that I believe my relationship with God to be my highest priority, my goal should be to ensure that it is reflected in the life I lead. Unlike my pie-in-the-sky #FamilyGoals, this is something I actually aspire to do. Knowing this, a quick glance at my schedule can be enough to put me in check. A calendar riddled with more work meetings than church meetings or more "go and play" than "stop and pray" is a huge red flag.

This is a real experience I had. I noticed that as a self-proclaimed man of God, I was very far from the ideal situation I said I valued. What's the trouble with that? I think you've gotten the picture by now—resistance!

As I said before, I hate reading—with a passion. However, once I learned that I could read the Bible on audio, I began "reading" other books, too. (That's the last time I'll put reading in quotes because I believe listening to an audiobook is reading just the same, but if you don't hold that same definition, just know when I say I read a book, it probably means I listened to it on audio.) So, I began listening to several books shortly afterward and was fascinated by all the new information I was receiving.

> *Straining is draining.*

One day, I took a look at my growing catalog of books and it dawned on me: if my value system says I value being a man of God, then I should really be reading the Bible. But I wasn't. Not even a little bit. What was my problem? Either it's not a true value, or I have allowed something else to take its place.

At first, I set my alarm bright and early. I'd pick a random chapter and hit *play*. When the chapter ended, I checked "Bible" off of my list and forgot everything I read. It was completed, just ineffective. As the days went on, I was hitting *snooze* more often than I was hitting *play*. Once I realized I had overslept, I'd try to make up for it and read two chapters, this time retaining twice as much information as before. (What's 2 × 0?)

It wasn't long before my lackluster attempts to be a man of God were causing me to come in late for work. I thought, *I could be a much better man of God if it weren't for work every day!* I even started to believe that work itself was of the devil. The kicker—I was working for my church.

When you live a life that does not match your values, you will either begin to fester with resentment for the life you live—which is the enemy of being content—or you will live out of your own strength, which will drain you of willpower. I was experiencing a little of both. It's far too easy to develop a victim mentality when we take personal responsibility off the table. Yet, we forfeit some of the most glorious resources when we think we're supposed to manage everything ourselves. I say, never be content with waning, but straining is draining.

The opposite is true. When you find out that your life *does* line up with those areas that you value the most, it adds to your self-worth and sense of purpose. There is also a mysterious energy you receive from feeling as though the things you are doing connect to your purpose in life. That's what we're going to aim for.

It's at this point that you ought to refer back to your list of *whats* and *fors* for everything. This represents who you aspire to be, so it shouldn't need many revisions. Over the years your list may change, but not much and not often. As we discussed earlier, from time to time, life and death experiences may change the trajectory of your heart, and these things will necessitate a change in priorities. I mean this in the most loving way when I say what really needs the most revision is *you*.

Please forgive me. I know this goes against the self-affirming trend where the most common platitude is "do you, boo." This destructive advice is meant to suggest that you should never make modifications because you are perfect, just the way you are. I'm sure you're a great person; I won't debate that. But you're not perfect. And you don't need a book to tell you how everything except you is the problem. So, if I have to be the bad guy on this one, I will.

It's inevitable. You will soon discover that your priorities are out of whack. Time is one of our greatest resources. If you take an inventory of your time—go ahead, inspect your schedule down to the minute, I dare you—it's not uncommon that the things we spend the most time doing happen to be some of the things we value the least. And vice versa: the things most important to us on paper hardly ever seem to make it into our calendars. This is an example of poor time management, since we're usually more effective at completing a task when we're passionate about it. We could get a heck of a lot more done in less time if we'd just do what we love.

Of course, it's never that simple. Instead of taking the time to get to know ourselves and respect our principles, we choose to give our best grease to the squeakiest wheels in our lives. Why? Somehow we've learned that it's an acceptable technique to get by in life. We're going to spend the rest of this book dissecting the idea of resource management and correcting poor praxis. But before we go further, we still need to address the rest of the question we asked in the last chapter.

DOES THIS EVEN MATTER?

You've determined the *whats* in your life. You've discovered the *fors* in those things you do. You've become a critic and ranked them from most important to least important. Now you have a Why List. It's pretty simple from here, right? If it's at the top of your list, it matters; if it's at the bottom, it doesn't. I'm not a psychic, but I'm going to guess that on your list was some reference to your finances, money, wealth, prosperity, income, or something like that. It's on there. I'm sure I'm right. But I bet it wasn't number one.

Where did money fall on your list?

Surprised? By the time we crack open a book on finances, we like to think that we have placed finances extra high on our list. People even offer us compliments at the sight of a financial book, as if it were a stack of freshly printed Benjamins. You can stop patting yourself on the back now—that's embarrassing.

If money isn't your number one priority, it should put things into perspective. There *are* more important things in this life than money. I'm not just telling you this; *you* are telling you this. You have weighed your values and you determined that some things are worth more than money. This is a perfect time to look at everything that comes ahead of it and assess whether or not you're giving adequate attention to those areas. Make a vow to yourself that you won't lose sight of these things in the pursuit of greater financial stability. Most importantly, don't forget to thank God for those things.

The items that come before money are all trying to tell you one thing: *No matter how much progress you make with your finances by your efforts, there will always be something you can do that will benefit you more.* That's a humbling thing to write, and I recognize how counterintuitive it is as an author to suggest alternative solutions when you'd think a book with "rich" in its title would be a strong advocate for financial success. Of course, as you read on, I will attempt to restore the value of a healthy financial outlook, and—for that matter—the value of this book.

Now, I've told you what topped my list as well as what didn't, but considering this book is going to cover riches, I guess it wouldn't hurt for you to know where finances ranked for me. I considered myself to be a money-motivated guy, so prior to completing my list, I was expecting money to rank the highest. Then, I started the ordering process and it felt absurd to place financial security above my relationship with God. For me, that's number one. You already know that.

Okay, so maybe money's number two.

No way it comes before my role as a husband!

Number three?

Not in front of my ideal character traits, such as generosity, charity, honesty, integrity, wisdom, and creativity.

Behind all of that, prosperity is what I personally chose to be next in line. It ranked number nine on my list.

So, does this even matter?

Yes, it does! Just not as much as I thought it did.

Don't get me wrong. I'm not at all suggesting that money

isn't an important matter. On the contrary, when we take a look at the top values of any person, there will always be an element of well-being. A large part of well-being is having the financial stability to live well. I'd even go so far as to argue that money is less of a desired ideal and more of a basic need. What I *do* mean to highlight, however, is the powerful lesson of reflection.

To continue the story of my mission to be a better man of God, I was feeling stuck. My most valiant efforts to read the Bible more were to no avail. And I was now beginning to look at everything on my schedule as an enemy of my passion. My job, music, basketball, date nights, Facebook, even church—nothing was safe. I was ready to cut everything off to make some progress. Talk about self-sabotage.

Conveniently, I received a message from my friend Donald, asking me if I wanted to participate in a Bible reading plan with two of my other good friends as a group. This plan was similar to the one I'd done years before, except in this one, we would read through the New Testament in thirty days.

For some reason, this lit a spark in me. There was a structure in place. We set up a group chat to discuss the chapters as we read. I knew exactly what I needed to read and when. Start at Matthew 1 and read up to Chapter 4. I always wanted to have something to share in the chat, so I made highlights over things to study and even cracked open my Bible commentary a time or two.

In reflection, I learned something about myself: I'm not a lone wolf; I belong on a team. When I'm held accountable, I'm unstoppable. As long as there was someone counting on me, I was faithful to the plan. When I was able to lift others up and be part of a team, feeling obligated to get a task done as a group, I succeeded. This wasn't news to me. My past experiences confirmed it, my personality confirmed it, as did my character and my values. My challenge, however, was self-discipline. That's never been my strength. Remember the ADD?

My wife, Kerri, is just the opposite. She is one of the most disciplined people I've ever met. I would say it's odd, but whenever I do she doesn't hesitate to remind me that she—in all her peculiarities—is exactly what I prayed for. I just wanted a wife who really loved God—is that too much to ask? But I feel like God over-delivered on this one; when I met her, she prayed and read her Bible every single morning. Of course, everybody puts on their best face at the beginning of a relationship; there's only so long I can pretend that fart jokes aren't funny. I figured once we got married and started living together, I'd truly see her habits come undone. No way, I was definitely wrong about this one. Dead wrong.

Every. Single. Morning.

Every. Single. Morning.

Like clockwork, she would open her eyes, sit straight up, reach for her Bible, and read and meditate for what seemed like hours. She put my best efforts to shame. But here's what I didn't know: her method was quite similar to mine. She'd pick a chapter or verse from some notes she took while in church, open to that page, and read a few paragraphs at a time. Then, she would sit and pray for revelation and understanding of what she read. At the time I started this new Bible plan, she was in the middle of the book of Matthew. She was devoting much of her time, but never felt like she was making much progress. Just like me, complete, yet ineffective.

As I was nearing the end of the thirty days, I began to anticipate what would happen when I no longer had the scaffolding of pressure to back my behavior. At the same time, my wife was taking notice of the progress I was making, seeing that I was completing more books than she was completing chapters. She spoke up.

"I'm really proud of you getting through that Bible plan," she said. "I wish I could make progress like that. I've always wanted to read through the Bible but I didn't think it would be possible or that I would remember anything."

Like music to my ears, I celebrated internally; I had just gained a new teammate! I opened up to her about my shortcomings when I tried to read on my own. She was asking for some of my confidence and administration; I was asking for some of her discipline and persistence. I started to make some modifications to the reading plan, stretching it out to about ninety days, and we invited our friends to join us as well. Every morning, whether I felt up to it or not, Kerri would wake me up and say, "I'm going to turn the light on, you ready?" It was time to read the day's chapters.

Every. Single. Morning.

Thank you, Lord, for sending me discipline when I had trouble developing it on my own. We got through this new plan and then quickly started another, this time beginning in the Old Testament. We finished it again the following year and again, each time adding resources, intensifying our study and discussions, seeing some passages as if they were brand new, and applying the reading each day to our lives. Our community of four has multiplied through the years but what is most notable is the power of God's Word that has multiplied in us.

I believe Donald's initial invitation and Kerri's humble request were both divine answers to my resistance. It's amazing to think that one simple link in a chat could set off such a chain reaction that would echo for years on end. To this day, we still pray and read from our Bible plan every single morning, and this practice has helped me grow tremendously in my top virtue.

But it didn't stop with my number one; it helped in my role as a husband—my number two priority. This one discipline is responsible for much of the growth in all the areas of my character that matter to me most. And it even has affected my view on finances and led to victories for our family in that area—which was one thing that prompted me to write this book.

So, why does this even matter?

Because your life has a unique composition—as represented by your list of *whats* and *fors*—which flows into your life's purpose. Regardless of how it ranked, every item on your list matters because that list represents you, and *you* matter. You matter to God and to the people you will reach when you begin to live out a life of abundant value. Hopefully, after completing and reviewing your list, you'll see that how you live matters to you.

Living a life that lines up with your values is a gift that keeps on giving. My example only highlighted a single, minor adjustment which made a great impact. Nearly every issue that you encounter is a conflict of your priorities. Sometimes, just knowing what your priorities are, having them written down, and keeping them readily available is enough to remind you what you need to do to keep from "doing you." It doesn't guarantee you freedom from life's challenges; it shines a flashlight on them and forces you to deal with them. But when you do come across a struggle or resistance, you can be sure that dealing with it will be worth it.

Even more than just the strategy for overcoming trials, lining up your life with your values is the catalyst for incredible opportunities. There's a phenomenon that occurs in the midst of introspection where one area builds off another area and so on. Nothing you do is one-dimensional, so every revision you make has consequences that affect more than one of your top values. When you start to see one improvement compound with the next, that makes it all worth it.

Take a look at your list again. There's one other piece I must mention. Remember, I predicted that somewhere in your list is the element of well-being? It *is* still there, right? I also reckoned that money is in some way a basic need. It could also be said that if you were to increase your financial well-being, you would have a greater capacity to positively affect every other area of value to you. That's a lot of power for one priority to have. That is why it is weighted so heavily against my other virtues. That is why one item so low on my list is worth writing about.

3

ENERGY AND THE UNIVERSE

*Since God has the only force
that can act in one direction,
whenever we do nothing, we
actually actively let things happen.*

If we consider money to be a basic need in the process of fulfilling our highest priorities, we're essentially giving it the role of a resource. A little more of it and our potential increases exponentially. A lot more of it and the possibilities become seemingly endless. It's puzzling how it works, but when our basic needs are met and our priorities are getting adequate attention, we often end up receiving additional resources in return that we didn't even need.

It's the whole "it takes money to make money" idea rearing its ugly head. Or how about this one? I'm applying for a job so I can gain work experience but I need work experience to get the job. *Hello, if I had work experience, do you think I would be apply-*

ing here? Or have you ever gone from being single and lonely to being in a relationship, when out of nowhere, a host of hopefuls decide to make their untimely intentions known? *Of course you're interested in me now.* Lastly, I've never understood this one. Why is it that the rich and famous, who can buy anything they want, are always given an exorbitant amount of free stuff: food, clothing, jewelry, event tickets, you name it?

I call this the resource paradox. For some reason, resources seem to show up for those who worry about it the least.

Is this an end to which we should be pointing our resources? We've already discussed how getting our priorities in order can create a mysterious energy in our lives, building tons of momentum and making it easier to accomplish our goals. This, in turn, makes life much more enjoyable. Now, I'm suggesting that if we could somehow gain access to enough resources, we'll be given all the resources needed to address our virtues in abundance. What is this crazy talk?

SHH ... IT'S A SECRET

I used this phrase—"mysterious energy"—in the last chapter, and it inspired me to name this one something more provocative. I felt the word "universe" would kick it up a notch. I'm a Chapter Title Snob, so right after I judge the cover of your book, I make a beeline straight to your table of contents and scrutinize the chapter titles. In case you are as bad as me, accept my apologies and my congratulations.

It's a bit disheartening when you realize that words like "energy" and "universe" can't be used freely anymore without warranting a glaring side-eye from your audience. These words—along with myriad others—have been hijacked by a movement of slithering charlatans armed with pseudoscience and a sweet-sounding sermon similar to Christianity but devoid of any eternal power. By enacting universal laws and sanitizing scriptures into an impotent impostor, they impress upon their victims all the intellectual and emotional benefits of spirituality without revealing the identity of the true spirit at work. It's not the Holy Spirit. Their increasing acceptance has come to be labeled "the

New Age movement," and all the words they commonly use now carry their stigma.

The theory goes, if you just think about it enough—whatever it is, really think about it—it will come to you on its own. Or that, by your power and the affirmation of the Universe, you can speak certain things into existence from nothing, thus, creating your own destiny. Sometimes, the emphasis is on vibes, and you are able to perceive outcomes of certain situations based on how you feel about them before they happen. All of these schools of thought come prepackaged with their negative counterparts as well: If something bad happens and then you remember having bad vibes beforehand, well, you were warned. Careless words could create something unimaginable and a bad reality is a product of your bad thoughts. Tell that to someone who has been violated or abused and they'll show you how cruel that is.

But there's a reason why this is popular. From the day we're born, we are all searching for a deeper meaning to our lives than just eating, sleeping, working, and dying. Some of us don't have to go very far and find all of life's meaning within. Some give up entirely on this seemingly impossible quest, while others of us recognize that everything we observe comes with a peculiar design that can't be an accident. From the workings of the tiniest cells in our bodies to the celestial bodies billions of light-years away, no detail has been spared. Whatever is responsible for designing a system such as this has to be bigger and more complex than the system itself. Is it a human? A planet? A solar system? A galaxy? No, bigger. A universe!

I believe the term you're looking for is: God.

The universe is the greatest thing we can understand; it's the entity in which everything we can fathom exists. To say the universe is amazing would be an understatement, but that still doesn't explain the idea that intelligent design implies a Designer and that universal law presumes a Law-Giver.

The God of the Christian Bible makes several claims to be this Intelligent Designer and universal Law-Giver for all we experience. The earth and everything in it bears His signature. Even abstract ideas such as soul, time, and love are said to have their beginning in Him.

But this theory has its caveats, too: acknowledging this God immediately obligates a response. Since the Universe is just a universe, it can't take any special interest in you, so every answer that comes out of its constant system can *only* be found in you. Shouldn't the One who designed the family get a say in how a family operates? Or how about the boundaries of sex? Shouldn't they be defined by their Inventor? Yet and still, there are certain laws—universal or natural laws—that have been defined by Creator God from which we all benefit. We all take gravity for granted, and we trust so much the uniformity of nature that when we remove the lids of our water bottles, we don't expect the liquid to pour upward. We enjoy mathematically calculated intervals of time: day, night; summer, winter; seedtime, harvest; football season, basketball season. And every person is a product of the great miracle of life (which I won't describe graphically); a law by which, essentially, we humans get together and make more humans through our humanness. (I know I just lost all chances that you'd book me for your birds-and-bees talk, but the actual concept is incredible!)

We get the privilege of experiencing these and other consistencies in life without having to first ask for permission. And whether or not we give credence to the God who continues to keep these things in order, we can expect that they won't be taken away from us. It's no surprise that some would want to use the principles of sowing and reaping or enjoy the proceeds of meditation. But like New Agers, some would prefer to sell you those free gifts with the designer label scratched off. The statements they make will often carry a reasonable amount of truth. The Bible speaks about the people who employ these deceptive tactics, saying it stems from sin and wickedness.

> They know the truth about God because he has made it obvious to them. For ever since the world was created, people have seen the earth and sky. Through everything God made, they can clearly see his invisible qualities—his eternal power and divine nature. So they have no excuse for not knowing God.   (Romans 1:19-20)

I'm going to go out on a limb and say the originator of this strategy was the serpent from the Garden of Eden. Yes, God planted this beautiful garden, placed the man and woman in it, and gave them access to every tree they could imagine—all except one. The serpent's strategy was to twist God's words, magnify perverse desires, and play on mankind's free will. In the end, however, it wasn't so much the serpent's lie that enticed Adam and Eve to take the fruit but their desire to believe the lie. They believed there was knowledge available to them that they could receive without having to trust God for it. This knowledge would make them like God (see Genesis 3:5). Then, they could declare the forbidden fruit a freedom fruit. However, the only environment that could permit them to be any more like God than they already were was outside of the parameters God defined.

It was sin then and it is sin today. This is a consistent theme of the Bible. Listen to Paul continue illustrating the repercussions of the movement in his day which sought to appreciate all the universe had to offer and put God beneath those things as if He were just another novel idea.

> They traded the truth about God for a lie. So they worshiped and served the things God created instead of the Creator himself, who is worthy of eternal praise! Amen.
> Since they thought it foolish to acknowledge God, he abandoned them to their foolish thinking and let them do things that should never be done. Their lives became full of every kind of wickedness, sin, greed, hate, envy, murder, quarreling, deception, malicious behavior, and gossip. They are backstabbers, haters of God, insolent, proud, and boastful. They invent new ways of sinning, and they disobey their parents. They refuse to understand, break their promises, are heartless, and have no mercy. (Romans 1:25, 28-31)

APPARENT DENIAL

Paul is saying that whenever we accept the benefits of a Creator but don't accept the Creator Himself, we're acting like adolescents. I recall going to a grade-school dance, which was supposed to end at 8:30 p.m. but my mom, being my ride home, thought 8:00 p.m. was better. Reluctantly, I agreed, but who really looks at clocks when they're hanging out and dancing with friends? About ten minutes after eight, my mom gave up waiting on me. She decided she would get out of the car, find the building where the dance was taking place, and ask a teacher where on the dance floor I was. The teacher came up to me, tapped me on the shoulder, then pointed over to my mom at the door—the only one of her kind in the building—and she escorted me out of the dance.

After a silent ride home, my mom and I discussed what went wrong at the school. I was supposed to be outside at eight o'clock. I shouldn't have made my mom turn off the car and come inside to get me. I knew I was wrong and confessed all of this to her. She quickly dismissed my confession, "I don't care about all of that. I figured you were too busy having fun to check the clock, so I decided to come inside and wait. But it was when you saw me at the door that I was hurt. You looked at me as if you were ashamed to even know me."

And she wasn't wrong. There was nothing more embarrassing to me than everyone seeing my mom pick me up thirty minutes before the dance was over. When I saw her standing in the room, the anxiety of my greatest nightmares hit the surface. I was glad I didn't have to walk home, glad to have a home to go to, but I just didn't want her uncool "mom sauce" blemishing my reputation. I considered the idea that she was my mother as just an irritating fact of life that came along with minor perks like food and shelter. And I wasn't alone; most of my peers who had decent parents wanted nothing to do with them.

Even though my mom clearly explained how much that hurt her, I didn't see what the big deal was until I realized I was doing the same thing with my faith. Have you ever been ashamed to boldly say, "The Lord God is *my* God"? I know I have. And

Paul lets us know where this disposition leads—a path of self-destruction. Every sin was included in the list, from things that should never be done, to sins that haven't even been invented yet, to disobeying your parents. If being embarrassed by the woman who had borne me could cause pain, how much more do I inflict on God—the reason I and my mom and the entire world exists? Furthermore, it's not enough to consider God an irritating fact of life; we either acknowledge Him or otherwise cause Him pain. How we feel about this truth reveals something about our faith.

> And it is impossible to please God without faith. Anyone who wants to come to him must believe that God exists and that he rewards those who sincerely seek him.   (Hebrews 11:6)

The issue of our faith is not about whether we believe that God is God; sure, that's a good starting point. But this verse shows there's more to our belief. Our belief also has an attitude ("I believe He rewards"). Our belief has a direction ("I desire to come to Him"). And finally, our belief has a responsibility ("I will seek Him sincerely"). With true faith, James explains that these should all go hand in hand.

> You say you have faith, for you believe that there is one God. Good for you! Even the demons believe this, and they tremble in terror. How foolish! Can't you see that faith without good deeds is useless?
> (James 2:19-20)

James is talking to religious people who felt like their job was complete by continuing the outward rites of their faith. But a belief in God ought to penetrate our hearts and influence our actions. For these believers, this meant they needed to quit showing favoritism and discriminating against other believers because of their social status (see v. 1). They couldn't just say a prayer and brush off people who were in need (see vv. 15-16). James is saying, "If you truly believe something, it should show."

The apostles weren't the only ones advocating for a belief that shows. In an address to His apostles, Jesus makes a jarring declaration about how the message is received in heaven when we despise being associated with Him.

> Everyone who acknowledges me publicly here on earth, I will also acknowledge before my Father in heaven. But everyone who denies me here on earth, I will also deny before my Father in heaven.
> (Matthew 10:32-33)

As harsh as it may seem, this is actually an act of judgment and mercy. It's oppression to force people to live a life honoring someone they want nothing to do with. There's a point at which God gets out of our way and allows us to have what we want. When our conscious behaviors reflect a desire to explore God's benefits apart from God Himself, we treat God like I treated my mom at the school dance.

If you've been guilty of this, you're in good company. Besides myself, Peter was one of the first to do it. When the time came, Peter favored self-preservation over association with Jesus. And then the rooster crowed. But there is hope in Peter's story; he repented, was received by Jesus, and later confessed his allegiance to Him. He went on to be a strong pillar in the foundation of the early Church and contributed to the Holy Scriptures. As long as you're breathing (and enjoying yet another perk of our God) there is redemption available to you through sincere faith.

So, what's the point? The concept of money management relies heavily on the existence of universal law. That is why there is an endless supply of books offering simple principles for handling money. But maybe there's more to gain if we place our focus beyond the universe and its laws and give all glory to the Creator of all. This can't mean just copying and pasting the New Age script and replacing all of the Universes with Jesuses—don't be deceived, their theories are only *based* on truth and are not true in and of themselves. In my opinion, the only thing worse than perpetuating destructive half-truths is doing so in the name of Jesus.

GOD FIRST

Hopefully, Jesus, Peter, James, and Paul have convinced you that Creator God has a place in your strategy to enjoy His benefits. (I also gave it my best shot.) If you didn't need convincing, allow this to be the reassurance that you're on the right path. Be honest, though; when you found out in the last chapter that my number one priority was my relationship with God, did you go back and pencil it into your list? There's no shame in that.

There's so much value in making your priorities list but not all items on your list carry the same weight. That is why seeing finances as a resource can place pressure on you to move it to the top of your list. The challenge of having your list acknowledge God is that it makes your faith a line item. Now it's comparable to money and competes with character. If it's not your top priority, the earlier sections of this chapter may have sounded like a pious rant. At least you were being honest. What's worse, when faith does top your list, you can become susceptible to the apathy possessed by the recipients of James's strong rebuke. James used the words of a common Jewish prayer to say, "Oh you pray this prayer? So what, that's not enough!"

It's not enough to simply write *do Christian stuff* on a to-do list and then check it off every day at lunch after you've said grace over your Chipotle burrito bowl. Sorry to break it to you. And there isn't any task you can add that can truly capture the weight of following Christ wholeheartedly. Yet somehow, because of the sense of pride we feel in thinking our motives are righteous, we settle for less every time.

Settling for less—what does it mean and what does it look like? It looks like offering God access to some or most areas of our lives but with limits. It looks like a desire to show others you haven't changed. It looks like harboring contempt for fellow believers. It looks like a lack of growth in character over an extended period of time. (See the topics covered in 1 John 3.) These are all a result of setting the weighty item of faith among the superficial.

Can I let you in on a secret? Here it is: money is a god. We don't like to admit it but it's the truth. Gods don't top lists, they're above them. They inform us of our status and provide us with the means to accomplish what we value. This is why we find ourselves evaluating each of the items on our lists according to how they serve (or defy) our financial goals. Money is not a value. God is not a value. They're both masters.

> "No one can serve two masters. For you will hate one and love the other; you will be devoted to one and despise the other. You cannot serve God and be enslaved to money."   (Luke 16:13)

It's time to ditch the God-first approach for a more fitting model. No, you don't need to go back over your list with a red pen; you just need to see it differently. In a Christocentric model (that is, when Christ is placed at the center), your faith is an element that you consider for each item on your list. There are no outright Christian tasks, but you can ask yourself how, as a follower of Christ, you should complete a task so that it may bring glory to His name.

It's the same thing we're inclined to do with money. Particularly when we lack financial resources, we tend to look at every activity according to its pay or its cost. It's difficult to write ambitious goals with this perspective because everything requires money. We find ourselves asking, "How can I do this thing in such a way that it will position me to profit?" If it can't contribute to the bottom line, it's a no-go. What if we exchanged that money-centric philosophy for a Christocentric philosophy? When you make this adjustment, you reject the god of money and Christ becomes incorporated in everything that you do, allowing the Holy Spirit to influence you in ways you would not have volunteered otherwise.

These little nudges from day to day make a huge difference over a lifetime. Remember, the goal is sustaining victories by continually allowing the spark of God's Word to have its way. Here we're presented with a unique opportunity to learn what God wants to communicate to us. In turn, we are taught to trust

God with His knowledge of every good thing. Often, you don't realize how far you've come in an area until you look back and there's no trace of your old ways in sight.

As I have journeyed through the Bible in recent years, I've been shocked countless times to realize that God cares about the little details. I've learned that the Word has much to say about our lives today, and contains a wealth of information on how we should live and how we should see people and circumstances. But the greatest lesson I have received is that the Word is not about us. And it's not about how we should live or people or circumstances. It's not about the world, or sin, or even salvation.

The Bible is a collection of sixty-six books written by forty authors over a span of nearly two millennia. While there are a handful of ancient writings out there, none line up in quality, consistency, relevance, and sophistication. But what really sets these writings apart from the rest is the unified message they tell. It's kind of like when the Mighty Morphin Power Rangers called on their dinosaur-themed machines—called Zords—to fight off space alien villains. On their own they were amazing, each having strengths and special powers. The real shocker, however, was that they could combine to form a giant humanoid robot called Megazord. This super machine was unstoppable and with a power greater than the sum of its parts, it was sure to thwart the enemy's plan to destroy the world.

I will not apologize for my perfectly fitting '90s reference; I'm quite proud of it. There actually are a lot of parallels that can be drawn from that Megazord example. But to drive home the point, while each book brings its own strengths, ideas, and stories to the table, it is when it connects to the others that it is most effective.

One of the greatest obstacles to really grasping this is the books themselves, especially the titles. (You of all people should know not to judge anything by its title, right?) Still, it's completely logical to guess the topic of the books based on their titles: the book of Joshua must be about Joshua; Ruth must be about Ruth; Isaiah about Isaiah; Daniel about Daniel. Those would be fair assumptions. And what do you get when you combine a robot Tyrannosaurus rex with a mastodon, a pterodactyl, and a group of other robotic prehistoric creatures? It would be fair to assume you'd get a bigger, more complicated robotic dinosaur. But it's just not so. While their individual novelties can be celebrated, they are best expressed when they join together—they retain their distinct attributes, yet now they resemble the likeness of a person.

The individual parts of the Bible contain a plethora of important stories but in actuality, the Bible itself *is* a story. And this story also reveals to us the likeness of a person. Yes, the whole of the Bible—the entirety of its sixty-six books—is solely about God and His love for us. It's about the Father. It's about Jesus. It's about the Holy Spirit.

> ## *What would it look like if the fullness of God's interaction in your life took human form?*

The New Testament reveals the person of Jesus Christ as the Son of God incarnate. As you read, there is a dichotomy continuously at work that cannot be ignored: Jesus was fully human, and yet, He was fully God. He is said to have been subject to all of the weaknesses of human flesh and even suffered the same trials that we all face, and somehow He endured without sinning (see Hebrews 4:13). Jesus was also divine. Paul writes a thought-provoking poem about this dichotomy to the Philippian Church.

> Though he was God
> he did not think of equality with God
> as something to cling to.
> Instead, he gave up his divine privileges
> he took the humble position of a slave

> and was born as a human being.
> When he appeared in human form,
> he humbled himself in obedience to God
> and died a criminal's death on a cross.
>
>   (Philippians 2:6-8)

Can you imagine stepping out of heaven—with all its love, purity, safety, and privilege—to step into the chaos of the world? It would take a strong sense of identity to exist in this world knowing you don't belong. Now imagine coming to that realization from childhood to adulthood. At some point, perhaps during His studies or maybe His spectacular baptism, Jesus was convinced He was more than just a man. He was someone the Scriptures had spoken about before He was even born. But Jesus didn't have a New Testament to offer this perspective; all that was available was the Throwback Edition—the classic OT.

The Old Testament includes hundreds of references to Israel's future Messiah, and Jesus was well aware of this. In one of His early messages, he implied that He was the fulfillment of these prophecies (see Luke 4:16-21). He even is recorded as hosting a Bible study specifically covering all of the verses concerning Himself (see Luke 24:27). The identity of Jesus provides us with a new lens through which we can more clearly view Old Testament scripture.

Most readers in the time of Jesus saw God as distant, limiting His participation in human affairs to words rather than action. That's not to say that they thought less of God; no, they considered His activity to be one of the most powerful realities, albeit quite rare. In fact, the phrase "the Word of the Lord" is used throughout the books of the prophets to refer to the direct involvement God chose to have with His people. Therefore the Word, in essence, *is* His essence. John was one who picked up on this in the nature of his friend Jesus and, like Paul, poetically illustrates this mystery.

> In the beginning the Word already existed.
> The Word was with God,
> and the Word was God.

> He existed in the beginning with God.
> God created everything through him,
> and nothing was created except through him.
> The Word gave life to everything that was created,
> and his life brought light to everyone.
> The light shines in the darkness,
> and the darkness can never extinguish it.
> So the Word became human and made his home among us. He was full of unfailing love and faithfulness. And we have seen his glory, the glory of the Father's one and only Son.   (John 1:1-5, 14)

John is using what his readers know about the Word of the Lord—that it is the essence of God's interaction with all creation—and making them ponder what it would look like if this idea took human form. John is saying *it would look like Jesus.* What would it look like if the fullness of God's interaction in your life took human form? I'd say, perhaps, *it would look like Jesus.*

As believers with a Christocentric approach to everyday life, we use the life Jesus lived as a model for our own. We also, as in John 1, get to have the Word of God in us and with us and creating through us and bringing life to us. And we get the privilege of knowing the Word directly, so much so that it coincides with our human nature and shapes our intuition. As the embodiment of the Word of God, every earthly thing Jesus did revealed something about God and His love for us. In the same manner, the entirety of our lives in every aspect is a reflection of our relation to the Godhead and His love. It reflects our relationship with God the Father. It reflects our relationship with Jesus the Son. It reflects our relationship with the Holy Spirit. This goes beyond acknowledging God as one and true, or Jesus as Lord; how we operate speaks volumes about this relationship, whether we intend to reveal it or not.

What does your life say about your God?

Working your way down your list, what do those areas have to say about your God? What does the way you are living out (or not living out) your values have to say about your God? What does your current financial picture say about your God? Are you beginning to see some areas of opportunity in your life?

Many Bible translations render John 1:14 to say *the Word became flesh*, which is faithful to the original text. But if I had started this chapter—with its controversial title—by saying the Word could manifest itself into human form, opening up the infinite potential for us beyond what we could possibly imagine, I might as well could have prepared myself to be burned at the New Age stake. We shouldn't shy away from diving into mystifying text; if it's in the Word (and in context), it one way or another expresses God's nature and we need not be afraid of that. When I read John's words, I'm so glad they are in my Bible, because I can boldly declare that this language is biblical in nature, belongs to my God, and can be rescued from the hands of New Agers.

To take it even further, not only did the Word become flesh, but if we allow the Word to become flesh in our lives, we can reflect the nature of Christ. And the resource paradox applies here, too: The more we apply God's Word to the things we do, the more opportunities we will have to participate in His will. By establishing Christ as the central theme through which all expressions of your life flow, you allow your life to become a Bible study for anyone to read. And many *will* want to read.

4

OTHER FUN NEW AGE STUFF

*The reward of great work
is not brief moments of
leisure; great work is the
reward of intentional rest.*

It may seem like I'm throwing a lot at you at once but because of New Age mumbo-jumbo, I'm working with a limited vocabulary. You probably understand this stuff more than you'll give yourself credit for because I'm really just talking about water to a fish. So allow me to bring some clarity to the resource paradox and the "mysterious energy boost" by breaking these down even further—and sharing more awesome analogies.

Have you ever thought about what energy actually is? As a kid, I was frequently told that I was full of energy. But what does that even mean? Everyone has energy in them; that must not have been what people were talking about. I think what they were trying to say about me was that I was very active and

I could stay active for hours on end. Apparently, I seemed to possess an abundance of resources that could only be envied, not matched. However, this "energy" was only evident to them when I put that resource to work. Therefore, energy, in this sense, is really just the result of resources being used. And any parent of a hyperactive child can tell you: just wait. His resource is not unlimited. Before you know it, you'll hear all the racket stop and he'll be spread out somewhere on the floor overcome with fatigue. Enter: the dreaded crash.

What happened? One moment, I'm running around in circles at Grandma's house and the next thing I know, I'm waking up in my bed the following day. I ran out of resources. The fuel (pronounced: sugar) that I shoveled down at Grandma's request and that gave me the resource to keep going and going was depleted by my activity. That's the first great lesson about resources—they're finite. We can use them as tools to accomplish our goals, but if we continue to do so without refueling, we won't see the desired outcome.

The second is this: the external tells us very little about the internal. Some of my relatives may have thought my running around was evidence that I was full of energy, but my parents knew the truth: my activity was evidence that I was burning fuel. We often think activity and output are good indicators of energy levels, so we choose to say busy. But being busy isn't the same as having energy—when we're focused on output, we're actually *using* energy. That's like saying as you drive along the highway, if you see a car on the road moving with the flow of traffic, then it's fair to assume their car is full of fuel. There are cars on the side of the road with a full tank while some fly down the road on empty. Seeing a car driving down the road tells you nothing about what's in its tank.

And nowadays, you can't tell which cars even have a tank. The age of alternative fuel vehicles is here, with nearly all manufacturers offering hybrid options. Many cars on the road are fully electric—meaning, they're powered entirely by batteries.

This brings us to the third great lesson on the resource paradox, regarding efficiency. Efficiency is the relationship between output and outcome. One of the major appeals of alternative fuel vehicles is referred to as energy efficiency. To put it in the simplest of terms: you can reduce wasted energy by getting the engine to take you further while using less (or no) fuel. Following this theory is supposed to save resources and money over time. If this is true, there are principles we can apply to our lives, and considering that pretty much everything we do requires an output of energy, efficiency is important.

One fascinating vehicle stands out to me every time I see it on the road: the Tesla Model S. This car is packed with luxury features, a sleek design, a huge touch-screen panel, and a state-of-the-art safety system that can sense the obstacles all around. It also has incredible performance features that rival some of the world's most prestigious supercars. Oh, and it can pretty much drive and park by itself. This car outperforms almost any car on the road, *and* it is fully electric. No gas tank, no engine, no transmission—that's as much as I know about cars, otherwise I would go on. But before the Tesla, I could spot an electric car from a mile away, as if the signature stamp of an electric car was that they were UGLY. However, the Model S was designed and crafted to beautifully and efficiently make a bold statement. Where energy efficiency is concerned, I believe the Tesla Model S can teach us three things.

0 TO 100 REAL QUICK

The top-of-the-line Model S has a mode (dubbed Ludicrous Mode) that can get you from a stoplight to cruising at sixty miles per hour in just 2.4 seconds.[4] No other five-seat sedan comes close. But strangely enough, this mode is only temporary. With something so out-of-this-world, why isn't it always on? Why isn't it the default setting?

Because starting is tough.

It takes more energy to get to full speed from zero than it does to maintain a speed you're already going. As a result, the batteries are drawing a lot of power, they get hot, and they degrade faster. You likely experience the same struggle. Are you a quick starter? I know I'm definitely not. But even those who are quick to get moving are using quite a bit of energy to do it. 64

percent of Americans require a cup of coffee every day[5]—mostly first thing in the morning. You just spent hours recharging your batteries and cooling your motors. The first thing you think of before setting out toward your wildest dreams is, "Coffee!" What are you really saying? "I need some starting power."

You're about to take on the world. Your to-do list looks a lot like a repeat of yesterday's—mostly because you carried over everything *from* yesterday. This is going to be a challenge. Have a sip. Starting power requires short-term use of highly charged energy. It gets you going quickly, but it's not very efficient in the long run. On to coffee number two—and it's only ten-thirty.

You've been running in Ludicrous Mode all morning, but rather than burning out, you've decided to keep fueling new blasts of energy with a fresh cup of joe. Besides the possible addiction, the health risks, and the expensive habit, the main concern with self-medicating is that you never address the real issue. What does this have to say about your God? If this scenario describes your norm, it says a bit about you and your motivators; you have a lot on your plate and you are determined to get it all done. But being Christocentric means you are not the focus in the Bible study of your life. It's time to turn off the turbo and get realistic about your resources.

There is actually a burst of energy stronger than any coffee. It's called willpower. Willpower stems from our deepest desires, and when applied to what we believe our life's calling to be, it can be a source of great energy to achieve heavy goals. But you want everything done on your list, so why not just apply your willpower and knock the whole thing out? Because that's ludicrous. Like almost all resources, willpower is finite. And if you want to go from zero to kiss-your-list-goodbye, you'll find yourself ordering a double shot by lunchtime, if you make it that far.

Running on the power of your will alone is unsustainable. And as Christians, we have a multitude of scripture references that appear to advise us not to activate our wills. We are told that the desires of our hearts come from our flesh, which is innately wicked (see Mark 7:21-23). The Bible says that we will always find a reason to justify our actions and declare ourselves right in our own sight (see Proverbs 21:2) so we can't even trust our hearts (see Jeremiah 17:9). But so many people are counting on willpower for their progress. Some are given strong personalities with a lot of willpower, some only have a little; regardless, the natural drawbacks are the same. Willpower is finite and a cold start can take everything we have.

TAKING THE HIGHWAY

You made it through lunch; it's smooth sailing now. All your meetings are out of the way, you've responded to every email, and your belly is full. Wait a minute—that third cup of coffee hasn't kicked in. You're dragging. You're irritable. You're thinking about the traffic on the way home and whether or not you'll be able to make it to the post office before it closes. Goodbye, willpower.

If you spent everything you had in your earlier tasks, the struggle will be real and obvious. But sometimes we find ourselves running on empty and we have nothing to show for it. When this happens, we need to evaluate our stamina and speed. The greatest enemies to our stamina and speed are the things that kill our momentum: distractions and the unexpected. Fuel economy ratings in vehicles generally test in two scenarios: city and highway. City mileage scenarios test the efficiency of a vehicle in normal city conditions, with lower speeds and traffic lights bringing you to a complete stop. We already discussed that starting is tough and takes a lot of energy. Well, stopping takes the momentum you built up and throws it all away. Good luck making it to the post office at this rate. Highway mileage, in contrast, assumes that you're traveling at higher speeds with fewer starts and stops. For this reason, highway mileage is almost always more efficient, giving you a greater outcome with less output.

Speed and stamina are two sides of the same coin. On the one hand, the idea is all about increasing the outcome. Speed is important because the less time it takes to reach your destination, the less time you'll spend burning fuel. On the other hand, we want to decrease output. Lower speeds burn less fuel and the faster you go, the more energy output it will require to maintain that speed. Higher speeds also introduce additional wear and resistance, which will make it even harder to keep your stride. The goal of stamina, then, is to maintain momentum by cutting through resistance. Stamina can be crafted—by design to reduce resistance and by processes to overcome it.

Tesla thought of this as well. The Model S has a signature design starting with a massive, flat battery pack that makes up the floor of the vehicle between the axles. This provides an even distribution of weight and a low center of gravity, both uncommon in its class yet essential to performance vehicles. As with most sports cars, the body is crafted with aerodynamics in mind, first cutting through the surrounding air, using the air to its advantage, and causing the excess to flow smoothly off its back. Finally, the car is equipped with a smart suspension, a process that lowers the height of the car's ride as the speed increases, minimizing drag.

Tesla makes it look attractive—but let's face it—cruising is boring. When you cruise the highway, you don't always *feel* like you're going somewhere. On the streets, the physical act of taking your foot off of the brake and putting it onto the accelerator and then back onto the brake again gives us the impression that we're earning our progress. That's the same reason so many people choose to speed out of control on the freeway. Either way, you're wasting a lot of fuel. There is a sweet spot, however, where the give and take is most profitable: cruising speed. You're making good time, getting the desired outcome, receiving minimal resistance, and leaving fuel to spare in the process. Check your speed, continually balancing between saving time and saving energy. Check your stamina, by minimizing distractions (design) and using techniques to adapt to the unexpected (processes). Find your sweet spot. And when you are presented with the choice between taking the highway or the streets, choose the highway.

REGENERATIVE BREAKING

You took my advice and ended up in rush-hour traffic on

the 405 on the way home. I'm sorry! One thing manufacturers rarely tell you is that their estimates are based on assumptions they make about average driving habits that they attempt to replicate in a lab. When they say highway, they're not thinking of the 405 or any other route in a major city during rush hour. If you're familiar with this type of commute, no matter what app you have on your phone or how often the radio station updates you on traffic, some obstacles are unavoidable. Things are going to come up that kill your momentum. There will be times when intermittent starting and stopping is the only option.

As unbelievable as Autopilot is on the Tesla, this last feature has one of the greatest messages on efficiency embedded within it. You see, on the average car, there's nothing you can do about wasted momentum. The brakes use friction to counteract the hard work the motor has done and bring your car to a stop. This friction turns into heat that is somewhat out of sight and out of mind. Tesla would say that's a bit silly. If a battery can send power to the electric motor which propels the wheels, why can't it work in reverse? What if when you weren't accelerating, the wheels could return that energy through the motor like a generator and recharge the battery? Tesla calls this feature *regenerative braking*. With this enabled, the momentum that the motors build up is never completely thrown away; it is turned back into a charging current for the battery to use later. A steady hill could even turn out to be a welcomed friend. So what could we learn from this?

There is more to the mystery of energy than just what is on the surface. To pretend that the only energy worth talking about is the kind where resources are being used up and put to work would be doing you a disservice. What if we had a built-in mechanism to recharge our batteries during times of limited activity? What if there were a way for us to fuel up any time we let off the gas?

I'm sure you get where I'm going with this. We do!

Have you ever stayed up all night working on a project only to review it in the morning and wonder who broke into your home and did sloppy work in your place? The mere fact that we can detect sloppy work in the morning that we couldn't the night before is a testament to the obvious. It is clear that the solution is to go to bed, get some rest, and pick up where we left off in the morning—yet we ignore our better judgment out of sheer stubbornness, foolishness, and pride. If we're going to get real about efficiency, we're going to have to put those things—and ourselves—to rest.

The concept of regular intervals of rest has been established since the foundation of the world. As part of the story of creation, Creator God essentially created rest.

> Then God looked over all he had made, and he saw that it was very good! And evening passed and morning came, marking the sixth day.
> So the creation of the heavens and the earth and everything in them was completed. On the seventh day God had finished his work of creation, so he rested from all his work. And God blessed the seventh day and declared it holy, because it was the day when he rested from all his work of creation.
> (Genesis 1:31-2:3)

Surely rest wasn't necessary for God. Unlike us, God has infinite energy and resources at His disposal. He could run in Ludicrous Mode for eternity if He wanted to. Yet seeing the full perspective of heaven, earth, and all creation, God prepared for the relationship He would have with the world and instituted the recharging mechanism for our benefit. He followed the same pattern as with the previous days of creation by looking over what He created and making declarations of intention and blessing. Rest is for us. Rest is intentional. Rest is special. Rest is set apart. *Rest is blessed.*

We know this subliminally because we live for the weekend. (And, oh, do we love our weekends.) At least we love the idea of not having to go into the office and sleeping in and catching up on rest. On a larger scale, we look forward to vacations and retirement in the same way, as if the rewards of great work are brief moments of leisure. What if I told you that great work was actually the reward of intentional rest? You might ask, *But how will I get everything done?* I think this is where our language has become a stumbling block to understanding the Scriptures. To us, rest sounds like inactivity, and if we're not doing anything, then nothing is getting done. The word translated "rest" in Genesis 2 is more commonly translated "cease" or "end" in other places in the Bible. For example, God used the same word when speaking to the prophet Ezekiel about updating his nation's tired mantra.

> "Son of man, you've heard that proverb they quote in Israel: 'Time passes, and prophecies come to nothing.' Tell the people, 'This is what the Sovereign Lord says: I will put an end to this proverb, and you will soon stop quoting it.' Now give them this new proverb to replace the old one: 'The time has come for every prophecy to be fulfilled!'"
> (Ezekiel 12:22-23)

God says He's going to shut that negative thinking down! To use the word *rest* in this way paints a more vivid image of how much of an action it really is. When we rest, we are inverting the function of our motors from delivering power to generating it. Do you realize that you have the ability to connect your brakes to your batteries so that times of rest will no longer be the enemy of productivity? Resting is an action. Coming to a stop is an action. Charging is an action. Breaking is an action. Even if we can't see it.

I'm going to call this *regenerative breaking*.

When we say we need a break, we are usually lying to ourselves. Because we're at odds with the idea that work brings progress through activity and activity through motion, we make an idol of idle time. But if you look at your list of values and turn those into short-term and long-term goals, you'll see that you most likely don't want to do *nothing*. There is an endless array of activities we would engage in if we didn't have to work, so our highest goal isn't being idle. Idling is what happens during rush hour on the 405—wasting both time and energy. But breaking is actively marking a season of effort complete while simultaneously preparing yourself for the next. In a vehicle, braking helps you get around corners, honor safe zones, and keep from unwanted damage; braking avoids accidents. In the same way, we navigate through the detours of life best when we apply breaks. Notice how, just like in the story of creation, rest isn't the goal itself but a part of the process. Breaking isn't just another item to add to your list of things to do, but a tool you can use to get those things done.

There are plenty of ways we can incorporate rest into our life's design and processes, but I will save the in-depth strategy for a later book. But regenerative breaking is not rocket science. **A good night's sleep** is one of the best forms of rest. This also means that early mornings (or for you graveyard-shift workers, the time immediately after you wake up) will be the time when you have the most energy stored up; plan accordingly. So don't have your job be the first thing you do after you wake up if it doesn't top your list. **Power naps** hold the secret to rest in plain sight; they are a great way to provide a quick charge when you need it. As with most forms of rest, naps work much better when they're planned. As few as twenty minutes could be just the attitude adjustment you need, while ninety minutes or more could get you through a complete sleep cycle and give you the full "power" benefits. **Pausing** is less common for workaholics but it is a very rewarding form of rest. This works best in a scheduled rhythm—like five minutes out of every half hour or ten minutes out of every hour, an hour out of every day, a day out of every week, a weekend each quarter, and a week or two each year—intentionally inviting a distraction for a limited time in order to decompress and take your mind off of constant output.

These types of breaks usually manifest themselves in the form of mandatory work breaks, holidays, and vacations, but I declare that you are free from the structures of these systems in favor of what works best for your priorities.

While we're on the subject of vacations, though, it is important to note that ceasing work isn't the only way to apply your breaks. Have you noticed that most people come back from their vacations visibly refreshed? And if you're forced to look at all their pictures, it appears as though they got a lot done while they were away. That is because some activities are like the steady hill, giving you more energy as you progress, sometimes even producing a net positive. Exercising is one of those activities. You'll often hear avid gym-goers claim that the more they go to the gym, the more energy they have. I haven't had such luck. One of the reasons for this phenomenon is passion. Passion is the currency you use to determine an effort's worth—it's the same system you used to come up with your values. When you're passionate about something, you're not concerned about what it will cost you to achieve it, but with the value it will add. You rationalize based on value and throw cost out the window. Remember the power of the will? Passion sips willpower and belches fulfillment. Above all, pursuing passion also says something great about the God who gave it to you.

God is a good gift-giver. As Christocentric believers, all of our passions are refined through considering the relationship we have with Jesus. And contrary to our bad reading of Scripture, His intentions are *not* for us to deactivate our wills but to surrender the power of our will to His. When we do this with delight, God gives us the desires of our hearts (see Psalm 37:4). He *gifts* us desire.

In fact, if I were writing in Greek, that word *gift* would most often be translated *grace*. We are conditioned to believe the word grace best describes God's pardon of our evil works. But grace is used throughout the New Testament as the power given by God to do good works. It's not just a perk; it's our heavenly battery pack.

Your willpower is limited, but when applied to delighting in the Lord, there is no more efficient use of fuel. Apply your will to the things in your life that will bring glory to the name of Jesus and watch how His power becomes a stream of life-giving water flowing from your heart (see John 7:38-39). And most importantly, use the gift of rest as a tool to refill your tank so you can continue to glorify Jesus in all you do. Discover activities that make more deposits than withdrawals on your energy and move them to the forefront of your priorities. As you break your goals into action plans, remember to make breaking a part of the completion process. Motion is not the same as progress, and until you rest, there is no end.

BUT DOES THIS CHAPTER HAVE AN END?

We've covered a wide range in this chapter and so much can be said about the resource of energy that it would exhaust the pages of the next few volumes in this series. Hopefully, this information has caused you to consider whether you are using your energy as an asset or a nonessential. At the very least, I want you to sleep on it. But regaining authority over your energy is not an overnight process; that's what I've noticed in my own journey. So what should be our ultimate end in the meantime?

Growing up in the '90s listening to hip-hop, I often heard money referred to as "ends." There were and still are so many slang terms for it that I never really questioned that one. It wasn't until much later that I learned to use the word "means" in regard to wealth and money. It dawned on me when I learned the difference between ends and means that we have the tendency to see money in either category. Oh sure, we'd never admit that we have set wealth-accumulation as the highest goal for ourselves (unless, of course, you're a '90s rapper). But the way we view work, education, politics, networking—even religion—often communicates our priorities louder than a rap concert ever could.

It's not a surprise that we could so easily confuse other ends and means in our lives. In fact, it's actually one of the continual struggles we face in humanity; we wrestle with what can be (means) and what ought to be (ends). That's what makes up the resistance gap I explained in the previous chapter. For every new ideal, especially the ones we receive with great emotion, we are tempted with a new end. *Now that I've heard this and believe it, I will make it my new motto to live by.* Pump your brakes for a second. Is this an end or simply a means to an end? Well, if you've bought into the idea that you ought to live a life that is Christ-centered, you have made one thing very easy.

Jesus is ultimately the only true end.

Doesn't that take some of the pressure off of you? You no

longer have the responsibility to correctly identify whether something has value in and of itself to be pursued with zeal. Here's a fun exercise: take your list of *whats* and *fors* and make yourself some lofty goals, both short- and long-term. Take some time to really get outside of your present state and dream a bit. Ask yourself, *If God really wanted to bless me in this area, what could happen?* This is what I call turning your *Why* List into a *Why Not* List.

A bit of a warning, it won't be long before a built-in alert system inside you goes off saying, "IMPOSSIBLE!" I'm not going to waste any time trying to convince you that your dreams are possible. All I'm saying is, *why not?* Your practical impulse may be right—how's that for motivational? But if you have an accurate portrayal of the values on your Why List, then your passion will value these dreams as worth the cost.

That's what I think you'll also notice: that almost everything comes at a cost. These dreams you have recorded are all miniature ends that you hope to one day achieve, but it brings up two questions. First, how in the heck are you going to be able to afford to make these dreams come true? The second question is the Christocentric one: *What does this goal have to say about my God?* As soon as you apply this consideration, you convert the dream from an end in itself into a means to the ultimate end of glorifying Jesus.

Say you have the goal of owning your own business one day; that is an end that is going to require some serious means. It takes money to make it happen. But say you get the means. Now what? Well, now you have a business. That was the end—literally. But if you instead want to pursue the heart of God through business, it changes the focus of your dream. Now that business is an opportunity to have autonomy over your time, energy, and financial resources. Now the more you earn, the more you can do to affect the poor, the homeless, the hurting, the broken, the immigrant, the orphan, and the widow. With your business, you can build structures, provide income opportunities for working families, and completely change your community. As with one of my friends in ministry, God may put specific people on your heart, leading you to give workers with a criminal record a chance. It doesn't end. You see, when Jesus is the ultimate goal, ends are endless.

And what about the means, you ask? Well, I think that's one reason you're reading this book. If you could just get hold of better financial strategies, every area of your life could be blessed. And since you'll have your priorities in order, you'll be able to be a blessing to others, too. After all, it is God's will to use His people to bless the nations, right?

Before we journey down that rabbit trail, consider this: even the ultimate end of representing Jesus to others with our lives is more than just an end. We are finite, but the God of the created universe is limitless. By using our energy to enact His will, He refreshes us and actually becomes the means by which we continue to pursue the means by which we continue to pursue the ultimate end—Him.

If that's not a blessing, I don't know what is.

But I'd bet a '90s rapper could tell me.

5

MO' MONEY, MO' BLESSINGS

If more money means more problems, then let me learn to be a better problem-solver.

I figured it was only right to pay homage to one of the most highly regarded rappers in hip-hop history—The Notorious B.I.G.—when I titled this chapter. His song "Mo' Money Mo' Problems" was released shortly after his death in 1997, and while us common folk can grasp the moral of the story, it never stopped me and other lovers of hip-hop culture from setting our sights on the cars, clothes, jewelry, and fame he rapped about. His philosophy only goes so far before it breaks down; in real life, virtually *every* problem I face can be solved with a little more money.

Sorry, Biggie, but I went there.

But it's nearly impossible to have a conversation on passions, desires, and dreams before we start talking about potential, effort, and resources.

MILLIONAIRE POTENTIAL

Here's what first changed my perspective. When my wife and I started using budgeting software, the service began with a free sixty-day trial. Not a lot happened in those two months—nothing significant for that matter—but I felt as though it would be a good idea to really nerd out before deciding whether to continue the subscription. So I went through every feature, inspecting every chart and graph, running every report. This is where I was caught off-guard. Nothing significant had happened, yet I saw a significant number that I didn't recognize. What was the number? The field was labeled "Total Spending."

In two months, we had spent so much money it made me do a double-take. *Wait, what? I didn't even know we made that much money.* Now to be completely frank, we were making a fairly average salary between the two of us, and because of that, what we spent was exactly what we made. At the time of writing this, the most recent census data (from 2018) plots the median household income in the USA at just over $63,000.[6] What could you buy with sixty-three grand? Go ahead, think about it.

And there's my point: stuff. Most likely, your first few thoughts were—for lack of a better term—stuff. When I saw our total spending for just sixty days, my first thought was, *Do I have a ten thousand-dollar car somewhere I don't know about?* If I spent all this money, why don't I have any stuff to show for it? It wasn't until then that I considered I've been eating my salary and pouring it into my gas tank and living in it. Every dollar we made was going toward something that kept our world functioning as we knew it.

My subsequent thoughts were more motivational. *At this rate, how much will we make this year? Do we need to spend this much to keep living what we consider to be comfortable lives? How much potential will we waste this year? The next five years? What about for the remainder of our lives?*

Now just to clarify: when I mention the median household income, the median is the point in a set of data where half of the population will fall above it and half will fall below it. But say we only focus on the half that falls below the median line, and say we narrow that down to an even smaller segment that makes less than half that number. This is just to use round figures, but let's say you were someone who makes an average of $25,000—that's twelve dollars per hour, full-time, the current minimum wage in my home state of Arizona. If you continued to make that salary from age twenty-five to sixty-five, that amounts to a total of one million dollars that will pass through your hands in those forty years.

As unlikely as the scenario above is—that you would make minimum wage for your entire career or that it wouldn't increase during that time due to inflation—the point I want to illustrate is that it's very likely you'll be responsible for spending over a million dollars in your lifetime. Recent data shows that the average American will make more than 2.7 million dollars in their lifetime.[7] With so much potential, I'm going to call you a *potential* millionaire. Now all you need to do to transform into a *real* millionaire is keep on living and stop costing money. Easy peasy.

In all seriousness, though, what do you plan to do if you keep living? How do you plan to spend your million-plus potential lifetime earnings? Companies across the globe are all fighting to answer that question for you. They want their product on your dream list. It isn't a wild conspiracy to say that Apple executives were strategizing how they were going to get you to buy the next iPhone while they were still designing your current one. They've spent your money before you even realized you were going to have it.

I needed that "Total Spending" eye-opener in order for me to truly consider what my potential was. Writing my *Why Not* list was like trying to pull out my own teeth. I have always been reluctant to write down any of my dreams because I figured I would want more than I had the potential to achieve in my lifetime. Therefore, I would either have to accept the fact that I would not be able to afford the things I wanted or that I would not want the things I could afford. The one thing that was certain was I could not both want and have, so my choice was just to not want.

With this newfound understanding of potential, I can have nearly anything I want; I just need to take control of either my earning, spending, time, or any combination of the three. Certainly, the easiest and the hardest of the three to get hold of is time. It's the easiest because unlike taking a second or third job or doing long division in the grocery aisle, waiting until you have money doesn't require any additional steps. But if you've ever hired a plumber—and been told to be available during one of those windows of time between 7 a.m. and 9 p.m.—then you already know waiting is a drag. Do you realize how long a day is? And it's going to take *how many* days to afford my dream car?

But sometimes we *can* get what we want. Sometimes we "luck up" and find just the right deal. Sometimes a loved one surprises us with a birthday or Christmas gift. Sometimes we fall into an unexpected season of good fortune, like when you magically get that third check on the fifth Friday of the month or when that well-timed tax refund gets deposited into your bank account. You can now officially have what you want.

#BLESSED

If you don't see that phrase a minimum of a dozen times per day, I envy you more than you realize. All the way from social networks into modern slang, we share stories about how we wanted something we couldn't afford but later became empowered to have that thing, then we add the hashtag "blessed" at the tail end.

Often, when I hear *blessed* or *blessings* being used, it's in reference to one of those impossible goals that someone wanted so badly. In these cases, the blessing is literally the money that is being gifted or discounted in order to acquire that thing. That's how you get things you want; you need money. You need a blessing. It's all the same, right?

Mo' Money, Mo' Blessings.

Besides money, there are other things we commonly refer to when we call ourselves blessed. *Blessed* can also mean that comparatively, you are exceptionally skilled or good-looking or intelligent. However, if you were to strip away the layers of elation, it would ultimately end up meaning you have received something that others may never get to have. If you're blessed, you are the object of envy—or at least you should be.

The idea of blessing brings with it the connotation that an experience was supernatural—literally beyond natural explanation. I've even heard it said, "God is in the blessing business." When we say that, aren't we just bragging on God about His come-through-itiveness? And that's a good thing, right? How else could we describe it?

Privilege.

I think the word most fitting with the way we use *blessing* today is *privilege*. A privilege is an advantage which otherwise would be regarded as rare that comes to a specially chosen recipient. The way we use the term *blessing* is practically synonymous with and can be used interchangeably with *privilege*, yet it is almost always applied to money and other material things.

BLESSINGS FOR SALE

I already told you I'm a lover of words who likes to nitpick over semantics as a hobby. Granted, and still, I feel it is my duty to offer you the challenges of adopting the "Mo' Money, Mo' Blessings" philosophy.

When a blessing is equated with money, it assumes the properties of money. Money is quantifiable; this gives a whole new meaning to "counting your blessings." Being currency, it also has a redeemable value that can be exchanged for goods or services. Although, if I were an advisor, I wouldn't recommend that you go into trading blessings in the Foreign Exchange market: I have witnessed folks declare one blessing at a billion-dollar lottery jackpot all the way down to a single dollar bill found on the ground—its market value is all over the place. Finally, as we discussed in the last chapter, because we'll never exhaust the list of goods and services we desire, money is seen as an end which is always good to pursue. Can the same be said about the pursuit of blessings?

Perhaps we have been sold a bill of goods on *blessings*.

How do you pursue blessings, anyway? What does that even look like? They transcend earnings, spending, and time metrics, so it's no surprise they hold great value to us. But it wouldn't make sense to dedicate our time and efforts to receiving one. Or do we value money earned by our labor differently than when it falls into our laps? Which one ranks higher for you?

Say you had two options: you could work to earn a living or you could enter a daily sweepstakes where you had a 1 in 300 chance of winning a year's salary. Those are good odds, right?

We see this philosophy play out on a daily basis, except the odds are far worse. Every year it seems there is a record-breaking lottery frenzy. Although it could be argued that the longer the game goes without a winner, there's a higher chance the next game will produce one, the truth is, the jackpot only increases in stride with its victims; kind of like a tally of suckers. And no matter how much we understand its unlikelihood, nearly all of us have a number—last week everybody else was crazy for playing it, but this week you'd be crazy *not* to play. You do it the smart way, of course; you only buy one ticket. "If the Lord wants to bless me, He only needs one ticket to work with."

I know I'm no better. Semantics aside, if a billion-dollar jackpot showed up at my doorstep and the Channel 5 News Team shoved a camera and microphone in my face asking, "How do you feel?" I know I would be a blubbering wreck, but if I could get any coherent words out, I'm sure *blessed* would be one of them, sneaking its way through my stammering. I'd be hard-pressed to find a better word.

Everybody has a number.

One billion-dollar check and all my talk about the value of earned income, controlled spending, and patience is thrown gently out the window. I guess I'm also in pursuit of blessings.

Now, if gambling isn't a moral deal-breaker for you, chances are something else is. Few of us would accept a bag full of money if we knew it was stolen from the bank. (Honestly, just the fact that someone would consider a bag to be a sufficient way to transport cash—yeah, that's definitely stolen.)

Never trust money that comes in a bag.

FINANCING BLESSINGS

But this brings up the second sincere concern: if blessings are the way we get what we want without working or waiting, what happens when something that isn't a blessing gets us there?

Of course, it doesn't have to be the aforementioned situations in order for us to assign that blessed title. In fact, I've seen a trend among my peers that is even more common than the examples I listed. In this trend, the spontaneous good fortune doesn't come in the form of finances, rather in the form of *financing*.

> The rich rules over the poor, and the borrower is the slave of the lender.   (Proverbs 22:7 ESV)

"They offered it to me with no down payment."

"It was ninety days same as cash—zero interest!"

"Look, they even threw in these accessories for free when I set up the payment plan."

What are they really saying? "I wanted a new car, but I couldn't afford the one I wanted. I went to the dealership anyway and further convinced myself that I needed to have what I was unable to afford. But in an excess of impulse, high pressure, clouded vision, and bad judgment, I decided it was best that I went into slavery to get what I wanted. But not the traditionally bad slavery—you know, this is the good kind of slavery. Sure it's bondage, but it's ninety days same as freedom."

If these peers of mine would put it in terms like these, I would feel much more justified when I respond with a blank stare of disapproval. Instead, I am pressured to say what I know they wish to hear after they've shared their celebratory testimony.

What a blessing.

That's the default response and they usually beat me to it. In these cases, the blessing is rarely attributed to the form of payment but instead to the item received, although I have heard some refer to the unusual terms of their loan as blessings. At this point, we have to come to terms with our understanding of Proverbs 22:7—if going into debt is akin to slavery, can it be a blessing?

> Be not one of those who give pledges, who put up security for debts. If you have nothing with which to pay, why should your bed be taken from under you?   (Proverbs 22:26-27 ESV)

This proverb can be taken so many ways, and is often interpreted as a warning against cosigning. But today, we often put up security for our own debt. In light of verse 7, it almost comes off as sarcastic. Can you hear the tone I'm talking about? You either have collateral or you don't. When you voluntarily go into debt, you are giving yourself over to slavery and allowing your possessions (security) to belong to someone else (the lender). If you're short on money, does it really make sense to give yourself and your possessions away, too? You have chosen to pay someone who already owns your stuff. You're giving away your own bed, and now the next dollar you make belongs to your lender.

Bondage is not a blessing.

It may seem like I'm coming down hard on anyone who has ever been in debt. Easy for me to say, just months removed from being in mountains of consumer debt. And it makes me think of the youth pastor—you know the one I'm talking about—who used to spend his teenage years drinking and partying and sleeping around, living it up. He's way past that now; totally sober, married, and holy. Now he's telling a room full of teenagers their lives will be a mess if they do likewise. It's awfully convenient that the last day we choose to tolerate a sin is the day we quit doing it. Can we agree that living in debt isn't biblically virtuous, yet completely understand why debt is so prominent? Is it possible to still witness to people about freedom even while we are in bondage?

God is powerful enough to reach His kids regardless of our present status, but the better question is this: will the people who read your life find two incompatible principles when they compare your approach to spending and debt with the truth of the Word of God? Will they find the fruit of your life matches the fruit of the Spirit (see Galatians 5:22-23), in this case, patience and self-control? I understand that not everyone is on the same page when it comes to getting out of debt, and many of us are content where we are, in the debt that we have. I didn't write this book to tell you that debt is bad; if you love debt, that is between you and God. What I do feel obligated to say is after scouring the Scriptures, there is little evidence (dare I say none) that supports the idea of debt *blessing* a person's life.

Bondage is not a blessing.

Can I offer you one more nugget on Proverbs 22:7? Have you ever noticed that we neither read the first half of the proverb nor do we read the whole thing together?

> The rich rules over the poor, and the borrower is
> the slave of the lender.   (Proverbs 22:7 ESV)

It's easy to read the second half and get the point: if you don't want to be a slave, don't be a borrower. But the first half is making the same point: this is someone you don't want to be. If you're steeped in American culture, you won't see it at first because we've idolized riches. Unfortunately, we have such a negative view of the poor that we read "the rich rules over the poor" and think "That sounds like fun!" and then we desire to be rich. Is it really good to be a ruler over the poor? Of course not! Lording over the poor should be as obvious to us as subjecting ourselves to slavery. We shouldn't desire either. This is the same sentiment expressed in Proverbs 30:

> Two things I ask of you; deny them not to me
> before I die: Remove far from me falsehood and

> lying; give me neither poverty nor riches; feed me
> with the food that is needful for me, lest I be full
> and deny you and say, "Who is the Lord?" or lest I
> be poor and steal and profane the name of my God.
> (Proverbs 30:7-9 ESV)

It doesn't have to be either-or. The goal isn't to be rich; it's to be rich in heaven. The rich in heaven acknowledge their God-given privilege and understand their need for God. They are a free people, and free people free people. Are you bold enough to ask God, "Give me neither poverty nor riches?"

6

UNDER PRIVILEGE

*Privilege is not a notch;
it's a nudge.*

If your life was a Bible study (and, in fact, it is), then these ideas should challenge you. The readers of your life turn a new page with every interaction. What are they reading? Is it any different than a cheesy infomercial? I'm being serious here. I've even heard blessing conversations come to a close with phrases like, "That's why I always make sure to tithe!" or "If you'll just pray, you can have it, too!" It's a setup for failure. I would never advise against prayer or giving, but I cringe when material wealth is used to sell them. The only thing missing is breaking it down into easy payments.

But wait, there's more.

This merit-based model is not only harmful on a personal level but also has proven to plague societies on a global scale. First-World Christians have been *notorious* in spreading this "Mo' Money, Mo' Blessings" philosophy. Historically, we often make the fatal mistake of looking at all the major accomplishments of our nation and calling them *blessings* (from God, of course).

We're not saying other countries aren't blessed, but check the stats—Apple, Google, Tesla, Chick-fil-A—do I need to go on? It follows that nations that lack or are unable to afford our developments are obviously under-blessed, and because the formula is simple—get money, get happy, get religious—they'll be sure to benefit if they try the process in reverse.

Oh, no! We're that zealous youth pastor.

What we *don't* say is as important as what we *do* say. And when we're not honest about what something isn't, we're effectively saying what it is. This is how a blessed society can show up with running water, electricity, and forced labor—I mean jobs—and really believe it is bringing a blessing. Is what we're not saying compatible with what God says? Many of these countries never would have known they weren't blessed had it not been for the brave missions of the West. And imperial motives aside, many of those missionaries showed up with the intent of doing the Lord's work. I wasn't there, but I'll go out on a limb and guess they didn't say, "You call that a house? Hashtag *lame!*"

No, we'd never say that! Not with our words, at least. We'd never say that we are the benchmark of the blessed. We don't say that others should look to us as the model of a blessed nation. But there is a certain posture stemming from the rich calling money a "blessing" that says it all. Could we be doing the right thing with the wrong heart?

Fast-forward to today's modern Social Networking Age and you will find many new opportunities to distinguish yourself from "everyone else." It's funny actually: with fabric woven from irony, one of the threads that all mankind shares is the innate desire to be unique. This common thread, the ego, is part of our human psyche—part of the "in Our image" design mentioned in the Creation account (see Genesis 1:26). I'm not saying wanting to be exceptional is wrong, but I am saying we have many chances to get it wrong.

Online, there is a marketplace of comparison. Our networks are filled with contenders with whom we can compare our lives. Do you realize how dangerous your smartphone is? At any moment, just opening your favorite social media app can set off hundreds of triggers for you. With every swipe, we evaluate and reevaluate our lives, placing an undue burden on our expectations of reality.

Recent studies suggest there could be a link between depression, anxiety, and our use of social media.[8] While it's not yet clear whether people at risk for depression tend to use social media sites more often or if the sites themselves contribute to depression,[9] it's worth considering what part we play in either scenario.

Often, the only people we get to use as examples to differentiate ourselves from are our closest friends and family. If our lives are on display, are our posts helping or hurting the vulnerable? This is where comparison gets messy; just as with the global issue, much of it stems from what isn't said. Sure, you're not *trying* to say that God places a higher priority on your prayers for concert tickets than He does for your friend Cheryl's rent money. Of course not—God is perfect in love for His kids and hears every one of their prayers.

At least, that's what your caption said.

Okay, granted, nothing is wrong with God. That must mean something is wrong with Cheryl. Yes, she's an ambitious single mom who was laid off last week. But she must not have been praying as hard as you, or maybe she should have been obedient and let that city bus merge into her lane like you did. It's about time your inconveniences paid off. Perhaps, she hasn't been inconvenienced *enough*. Realistically, Cheryl just needs a three-week buffer, enough time to start her new job and get her first paycheck. You could go shopping with her for a new work outfit and cover the cost. Or hey, inviting her and the kids over for a meal would be nice. Honestly, almost any move you make to show you care would comfort her, but what she doesn't need is a Job's comforter—your twisted definition of *#Blessed* isn't helping.

But you've got Beyoncé tickets.

Is that where you draw your line of consideration? Realize that I'm only saying this because you'll probably never hear it from Cheryl. Good friends aren't going to rain on your parade (or your concert), even when they could use a leg up.

I'm not calling you a bad friend. I know you've thought about this before because you've been on the receiving end, too. With social media, ideas are constantly run through the filter of what somebody else thinks—either what we think others will think, or what we want them to think, and what we think about that. When it happens to you, (oh, and it happens) all of these ideas are constantly at war with your own belief systems.

Social media defines blessings for us more clearly than our Bibles. We see people use the hashtag *blessed* ten times per day when they get a free drink, some new clothes, a tank of gas, a new car—all blessed. So whether we agree or not, all of these things are blessings. When they have a good hair day or feel they look good, they say, "I'm blessed." And it's in these things that we go, "That's what blessed is."

We ought to consider how we might be contributing to someone else's redefinition of blessing. We can be damaging their understanding of blessing by exalting our own. In their eyes, how might this other person's definition of blessing be shifted away from God's by following you online? The more you participate, the more dangerous the implications become. It's a very real consideration that we should take.

ONE SHOT

When I see people abusing the word *blessing*, I think of Matt, my high school basketball teammate. He was a great player but he struggled academically and disciplinarily. Because of his grades, he was unable to even suit up for the first five games of the season. Finally, in the sixth week, his grades showed signs of improvement and he could wear the uniform for the first time—but because he let his temper get the best of him in practice, our coach told him he couldn't start until the second half of the game. He patiently occupied the bench until halftime, seemingly content just to know each second would be a moment closer to his time to shine.

At the half, he was eager to speed up the locker room pep talk; he still hadn't touched the court. He was limbering up as if the game was just beginning—and for him, it was. But when he finally got the chance to warm up, you could just tell he was on fire—he couldn't miss. The time for his debut had arrived and he was ready to put on a show, making up for six weeks of basketball in just twenty minutes.

The whistle blew and Matt ran straight to the inbounder who passed him the ball. As soon as the ball touched his fingertips, the game went into slow motion. Everyone in front of him cleared out of his way, revealing a wide-open goal from three-point range. He shoots. Swish. Matt jumped and raised his fist in excitement as the entire gym keeled over in laughter.

Great shot. Wrong hoop!

A fun fact I learned that day and the silver lining to the story: even if you shoot a three-pointer, the other team only gets two points when you score in your own goal. Needless to say, Matt suffered a great deal of embarrassment, while the rest of the team, myself included, shared crippling fits of hilarity.

Of course, when we do this with God's blessings, it's no laughing matter. When blessings are equated with prosperity, the focus is far too often placed on the "stuff" we got. And sometimes, we rightly attribute our blessings to God, but since we feel like we're on fire and can't miss, we place the focus instead on how hard we worked or how long we prayed or why we deserved it so much. These are all shots taken against our own goal.

This directly goes against the purpose of the Bible study of your life—to introduce readers to the Ultimate End, who is greater than you. And, if you're being honest, you don't want that kind of pressure, anyway. Do you really want to be responsible for ensuring the earth continues to rotate counter-clockwise? (Full disclosure: I have no idea which direction the world turns. See, it's a good thing I'm not God. Point proven.)

CONSIDERATE—A PRIVILEGE

If you're anything like me, you've already begun to feel the weight of responsibility that comes with adopting a Christocentric worldview. And adding in the consideration of others makes my pursuit of happiness way too complicated to walk out in a few easy steps.

I told you we were going on a journey.

As much as I'd love to offer a simple solution to these challenges, the truth is, we already have one. Jesus answered the "most important" question from Chapter One this way:

> And he said to him, "You shall love the Lord your God with all your heart and with all your soul and with all your mind. This is the great and first commandment. And a second is like it: You shall love your neighbor as yourself." (Matthew 22:37-39 ESV)

With this reminder of Jesus's words, it's clear we have all been guilty of aiming at the wrong hoop at times. And the truth is, most of us are great shots. Regardless of what you've written down or resolved to do as a result of reading this book, this is the only goal that counts. This is our goal.

The items on your Why Not list aren't actually goals: they're ways to score; they're shots. Your business is a shot. Your dream home is a shot. Your Beyoncé tickets ... are a shot. When the opportunity comes your way, it is up to you to find a way to use these shots to score some points. Again, the solution is not changing the mechanisms of our shot; rather, we just need to take aim at the true goal we already have.

Practically, this looks like reminding yourself weekly, daily—as often as necessary—which direction you're supposed to be facing. It's easy to get turned around in the game of life. We must make a habit of going before God in prayer, which consists of opening our hearts to God as well as listening to the Holy Spirit. We can expect that God will remind us of our ultimate end (see John 14:26).

Although the word suggests a looking-back, the purpose of a reminder really lies in what's ahead. This means that any new desire or opportunity can and should be run through a filter into one of your top values. We already do this inside our heads before we make a decision, except we also take into consideration all the things that cloud our vision and get in the way of living according to our values—you know, like other people and their modern definitions of *blessing*.

Need I remind you of this: the way we use the word *blessing* today is just a hip way of saying *privilege*? Saying something is a blessing should invoke a sense of obligation to give honor to God. After all, bondage aside, that is where blessings come from, right? Likewise, calling something a privilege should indicate to us that we have a responsibility. *Why not* use these God-ordained advantages to assist those who are less fortunate?

In Luke 10, immediately after Jesus explains the great commandment, He is challenged with a follow-up question: *Who is my neighbor?* Jesus responds with the story of the Good Samaritan.

> Jesus replied with a story: "A Jewish man was traveling from Jerusalem down to Jericho, and he was attacked by bandits. They stripped him of his clothes, beat him up, and left him half dead beside the road.
>
> "By chance a priest came along. But when he saw the man lying there, he crossed to the other side of the road and passed him by. A Temple assistant walked over and looked at him lying there, but he also passed by on the other side.
>
> "Then a despised Samaritan came along, and when he saw the man, he felt compassion for him. Going over to him, the Samaritan soothed his wounds with olive oil and wine and bandaged them. Then he put the man on his own donkey and took him to an inn, where he took care of him. The next day he handed the innkeeper two silver coins, telling him, 'Take care of this man. If his bill runs higher than this, I'll pay you the next time I'm here.'
>
> "Now which of these three would you say was a neighbor to the man who was attacked by bandits?" Jesus asked.
>
> The man replied, "The one who showed him mercy."
>
> Then Jesus said, "Yes, now go and do the same."
> (Luke 10:30-37)

I wouldn't dare tell Jesus He didn't answer the question, but do you see what He did? It isn't about who is a neighbor *to me*—only who will I be a neighbor to. And if you think being a neighbor is tough, imagine comforting someone who despises you—and then paying for their restoration and covering their hospital bills. Yes, loving your neighbor like this is costly. Perhaps you need a reminder of the state you were in before Jesus got your attention. Perhaps you could use a reminder of the time your heart denied or downright despised your Savior. Perhaps you need to be reminded of what it cost to restore you.

Perhaps Jesus did just that.

> We know what real love is because Jesus gave up his life for us. So we also ought to give up our lives for our brothers and sisters. If someone has enough money to live well and sees a brother or sister in need but shows no compassion—how can God's love be in that person?   (1 John 3:16-17)

If I were to use my privilege toward the end of loving someone else who is underprivileged, what's in it for me? What if I put it another way: is there a benefit to using the blessing I've received as a way of bringing a blessing to someone who needs one? I bet that's beginning to sound familiar now. In Paul's farewell to the elders of the church at Ephesus, he gives his own reminder.

> And I have been a constant example of how you can help those in need by working hard. You should remember the words of the Lord Jesus: "It is more blessed to give than to receive."   (Acts 20:35)

Note here how Paul presents his life as an example—like a living Bible study. He connects the means of his common work to the end of helping the less fortunate. And finally, he reminds us of the direction we're supposed to be facing, using the words of Jesus.

It's almost like Paul got an advance copy of this book.

Blessing is *the blessing.*

These words of Jesus, by the way, must've been something everyone knew He said because they're not found elsewhere in Scripture. But the saying is nonetheless remarkable. *Giving is where "Mo' Blessings" come from.* You've probably heard the saying, "We're blessed to be a blessing." And it's so true. I like to put it this way: Blessing *is* the blessing.

"MORE" PROBLEMS

According to Jesus, the way to *more blessing* is giving what you have away. Now this, I can say, is an end which is always good to pursue. How does it work, though? Only in an upside-down Kingdom would giving away be a path to receiving more. But perhaps our desire for money isn't the real problem; maybe it's just the symptom. I think the most significant problem with *blessing* is the problem of *more*.

The annoyance of using *blessing* and *money* interchangeably could just be written off as an argument of semantics up to this point. But money and blessing are incompatible in the sense that we can confirm it's good to pursue more *blessing*. We do that by using what we have to serve those in need. That literally *is* our *privilege*. The way to experience *more* is by giving *more*. (The jury is still out on more money.)

Almost everything I can dream of can be achieved with more money. Everything except contentment. And simple mathematics proves that giving money away means I will have less. Even when I take into account my natural potential, I can definitively say I could use more earnings, I'd like to spend more, and if I had more time, I'd probably use it to make more money so I could spend more. Something about more money always leads to a *more* problem.

Man, Biggie was right all along.

This hunger for what you're already full of is something the Bible often refers to as the sin of gluttony. It's commonly understood as the constant desire for excess, but I think it's better described as the insatiable desire to meet a mistaken priority. The trouble is this: as long as we are counting on our dreams and goals to bring us fulfillment, we will continue to be the *needy*, not the *privileged*. We find ourselves asking, "Who will be a neighbor to me so I might love them?" instead of considering love for others as the blessing. Gluttony comes when we're both the *blessed* and the *needy* at the same time.

You told me to dream, I hear you saying. *You told me to ask, Why Not? Now, are you trying to tell me I'm a glutton? That sounds like a pretty good reason why not right there!*

Don't worry, I would never say that ... directly. I'm saying the world wants you to be a glutton—less and less satisfied with every dream the Lord permits you to accomplish. We essentially allow *more* to be the measure of our satisfaction. But *more* is not a measure. And even as we uncover this problem (when our goals don't meet our impossible expectations) we tend to chalk it up as necessary for living "the good life"—First World problems. We just accept this *more* problem and then resolve to be better problem-solvers. This concept—sometimes dubbed "the law of diminishing returns"—is not something you just have to accept. There is a way to be content while remaining passionate about your dreams of more.

But is that way *good*?

7

MY GOODNESS

*Anything belonging to this
world is subject to gravity.*

If you had to choose, which would you say is better: one car or five cars? What's better: one acre of land or ten acres? Five dollars or five million dollars?

Easy, right?

It's easy because in each question there's a glaringly obvious right answer. The only reason you wouldn't choose the second option is if you thought it was a trick question. There's no question that we'd all prefer five million dollars over five dollars; let's just skip right past that one. But the others don't take much thought, either. What could I do with ten acres? I don't know, but I'm sure a whole heck of a lot more than I could with one acre. I'm going with ten—final answer. And something within me is fixated on the idea of sporting a different vehicle each day—I'm even willing to rough it on the weekends like a one-car peasant.

Considering none of this reasoning is giving you a new revelation, I'm sure you're beginning to grow suspicious of the questions I asked. So what's the trick? Well, firstly, I asked a terribly framed question—that was totally my fault. But you most likely didn't notice the real question being asked because our normal everyday language finds no faults with the way I framed it. What I asked was "Which is better?" but the gut reaction is to answer a different question altogether.

When I ask you to choose which option you consider better, I'm asking you to evaluate them on the parameter of goodness. But since both of the options I gave you seemed good to you, you are led to assess *how good is this thing?* That's when comparatives come in.

Let's talk grammar for a second. *Good* is a positive adjective in its most basic form. While an adjective helps describe a thing, a comparative expresses the same sentiment but takes it to the next level. A superlative trumps them all, indicating the maximum level of that description has been reached.

For the positive *good*, the comparative is *better* and superlative is *best*. If you were going to describe something as better than something else, it's because you believe it will bring a level of goodness beyond the other option presented. Unless, of course, you were answering a trick question.

Before we can make any assessment on *better*, we'd better know what *good* is. We are all born with a barometer of goodness, constantly venturing toward what we believe is right and good. And as we collect new experiences which we deem good or bad, our idea of goodness gets revised over and over again. We realistically carry thousands of references which we can use to determine if we think something is good or not.

And then we come to God. This is where we believers face some conflict. We have preconceived "good" feelings in our bodies and "good" ideas in our minds along with a "good" for every other sense: taste, smell, sound, and sight. Yet we know that God is good and are told the definition of good comes from God. And our Bible shows that God had a solid grasp on *good* from the very beginning.

> Then God said, "Let there be light," and there was light. And God saw that the light was good.
> (Genesis 1:3-4a)

Yes, Genesis holds the key to understanding goodness. God saw something in the light. Later, He saw something in the order of the land and seas; He saw something in the growth of vegetation; He saw something in the rhythm of day and night; He saw something in the population of the heavens; He saw something in the swarming fish of the sea and the soaring birds of the air; He saw something in life on earth. He saw goodness.

> Then God looked over all he had made, and he saw that it was very good!   (Genesis 1:31a)

From Genesis 1:1, the story begins with something—the heavens and the earth. But we quickly learn that the earth "was formless and empty, and darkness covered the deep waters" (v. 2). This description is used elsewhere to describe uninhabitable wilderness and unnavigable sea. To put it another way, the earth was not fit for human life as we know it. The subsequent verses paint a visual picture on this turbulent backdrop through poetic repetition. For instance, God's creative act of bringing light was His first step in bringing order to this formless chaos. We see throughout Chapter 1 that God sees goodness where His crafted order enters and when life is cultivated. We gather from this account of creation that goodness is directly related to the quality of order and the value of life.

In a sense, it's similar to the way we define the word today; *good* is a word that expresses the value brought by or the quality of a thing. Yet what happened in Genesis 3 continues today—our definition of good is getting shaped by external influences which are opposed to God. Any and every time we seek to refine our definition of good apart from God, we follow the ministry of the serpent. This ministry has always taken an interest in twisting words around.

THE GREAT CONFUSION

So which is better? One car or five cars? One acre or ten acres? Five dollars or five million dollars? Here's the twist. The moment you're given numbers, your brain shifts from assessing the quality to assessing the quantity. Five is obviously greater than one, and so is ten, but five million is even greater than both of those. But does that mean it's *better*? No, it simply means it's *greater*.

We mix these words up all the time because we share the problem of *more* discussed in the last chapter. Because we believe *much* is *good*, we also believe *more* is *better*. And if more is better, then *great* must be a level above and beyond *good*. Now I hear it in every competition television show or anytime someone wants to give me their verbal Yelp review: "It was *good* but it wasn't *great*." So in our minds, it's not *good, better, best*; it's *good, great, awesome*. (Everybody has their own pinnacle word; mine is "awesome"—as long as yours isn't "epic," we can still be friends.)

The tension between *good* and *great* is also evident in conversations about the "GOAT." No, I don't have regular chats about my favorite curry dishes. Many of the arguments about who is the "greatest of all time"—whether it's in music, sports, or entertainment—boil down to skills versus impact. Some judge based on talent within their field while others judge based on overall accomplishments. Often, the most gifted ball players have not belonged to teams who have won championships, just as the most talented musicians don't have the Grammy Awards or album sales to back them up.

Good and great are two related yet distinct words meant to highlight two different attributes. Goodness is the measure of quality and value. It communicates benefit, wellness, and morality. Greatness is the measure of quantity and size. It communicates power, influence, and importance. God is wholly good and God is wholly great, and the two are not the same. It's when we settle for *greatness* on our quest for *goodness* that we forfeit experiencing one of God's premier attributes. We can't afford to continue confusing the two.

Let this sink in: *greater* does not mean *gooder*.

Have you ever gotten a gift you can't afford, like a puppy or a garden? I know this sounds absurd, but if I were given five free cars today, I wouldn't be able to afford it—not to drive them, anyway. Firstly, I'd have to register and get plates for each car.

Then, I'd have to make sure they all have insurance. There's no way I could justify paying an amount several times my cost of housing in an effort to have more cars than I need. And where would I park them? (I know someone is scoffing right now, saying that I should sell them or start a transportation business; you like to ruin kids' Christmases, too, don't you?) What I mean to say is, simply having a starting lineup of vehicles doesn't instantly add any value or quality of order to my life. Like that new puppy, it's a great idea but, in fact, it comes with a level of responsibility and expense that actually does the opposite.

Greater changes the dynamic. Is it really better to have five million dollars if it means it will cost you the relationships between you and your family and friends? (And no, Grinch, we are not going to buy new friends.) If you're still having trouble grasping this concept, try substituting dollars for something at the top of your list that you love—like your spouse or your kids. At what point is *greater* no longer *better*? Five million spouses? Five million kids? But what do I know; you might be right. Perhaps having five million dollars is not just greater but also better for you. But did you even stop to think about it? Of course not! It was a no-brainer.

> ## The Kingdom of Heaven is not a no-brainer.

This is geometry class all over again. Sometimes, I would ask my classmates for the answers; sometimes I would consult my handy graphing calculator; and other times, I could figure out a problem in my head. But even if I came to the right solution, it wouldn't count unless I could show my work. This was so frustrating as a student—*You asked me to solve a problem, then why are you not satisfied with the correct answer?* My teachers would always say it was to prepare me for the real world, where shortcuts can cause more headaches than they're worth in the long run. So they instructed me to "show your work" to see if I was using the proper formulas in the right order.

I know it's frustrating, but I'm going to ask the same thing of you right now. The Kingdom of Heaven is not a no-brainer. Your path to the answer is just as important, if not more important, than you having the right answer alone. If more is better, are you able to show your work? How did you come to that conclusion? Where does God fit into all this?

The bottom line: God sets the standard of good, not us. That's the formula we're choosing to use as Christocentric believers.

So ... is money good? Is it bad? How can we really be sure, except to ask the Definer of good Himself? It seems ridiculous to ask whether money is a good thing, but we've identified that we are all susceptible to a "more" problem when we make wealth an end. Maybe there is something about money that inherently lures us into this trap.

Money is definitely important—there's no two ways about it. As I pointed out earlier, having more of it means we could do more good, but why is it that so many—especially those who have the most of it—seem corrupted by it? We've decided to go to God for the answer, and what better way to hear from Him than to see what He has already said in His Word?

If you just do a word search in the Bible, you will get thousands of results for passages related to money. In his book, *Your Money Counts*, author Howard Dayton identifies 2,350 verses related to money and possessions.[10] We know a lot of them by heart, but what do they really say?

Well, I've got good news: the Bible says some really good things about money. Here's one for you, "The Lord will give you prosperity ... you will lend ... but not borrow" (Deuteronomy 28:11-12). Proverbs 10:22 says, "The blessing of the Lord makes a person rich and he adds no sorrow with it." I think we can drop the gavel right here. Money is good. Case closed?

Not so fast.

There are also some negative things the Bible has to say. We all know this one: "the love of money is the root of all kinds of evil" (1 Timothy 6:10). Yes, *all* kinds of evil. Jesus taught that "the cares of the world and the deceitfulness of riches and the desires for other things enter in and choke the word, and it proves unfruitful" (Mark 4:19 ESV). And let's not forget about the words of Christ which inspired the theme of this book: "It is easier for a camel to go through the eye of a needle than for a rich person to enter the Kingdom of God!" (Mark 10:25). Riches can keep you from heaven!

So, it sounds like the Bible is all over the place—sometimes money is good, sometimes it's bad. Are these contradictions? Not at all! If we're honest, there have been times in our own lives when money has been a blessing to us and other times when it has been a distraction.

THE GREAT COMMISSION

I recall a time when I was down to my last few bucks—I'm talking too broke for an ATM—and had resolved to go without lunch for the day. (As some put it: involuntary fasting.) A friend came along and suggested we go to lunch, which I politely declined, and then he responded with the magic words, "I'm paying." Hashtag blessed.

I was working in sales at Guitar Center, and much of my income was commission. I was always known for being laid-back, honest, friendly, and a good listener; all nice ways of saying "not a good salesman." I prided myself on never selling someone an item they didn't need and making sure they didn't pay more than they had to. As a result, I'd always linger around the middle third of sales rankings.

The last day of this particular month, however, a huge deal landed in my lap which brought me to the top of my department and within dollars of being ranked number one. In walked one of my most loyal customers just looking for some headphones before heading out to a gig that night. I found myself pulling up a list of all the headphones and how much profit they would make me—an instinct I'd never had before. I made number one that month, and my incentive check was sizably above average. I even received a "Most Improved" plaque in my honor, which may as well have said, "Finally, you don't suck." (We've got to do better with those Most Improved awards.) It was for other reasons, though, that I never felt good about it. All I did was sell a friend some headphones he fell in love with. But I told him they were better headphones, because it was better *for me*. I fell victim to the numbers and exchanged good for great.

Chances are, you're a better human than me but you've still had experiences like these. The elation when someone *actually* pays you back, the hunger for higher commissions, the bitter-sweet spoils of your long-overdue promotion—a pay increase comes with whispers through the hall. "Look, here comes so-and-so, did you hear she got that promotion? I wonder what she did to get it." It's one thing to let people throw their own "petty party" but when rumors fly, especially from former teammates, it can be hard to combat. And it's a tragedy when lunch-break buddies become the most boisterous offenders of awkward silence in the break room. The reality is that the Bible speaks of it all: the good, the bad, and the ugly.

If our goal is to discover a bunch of Bible verses that match our current outlook on money, that's a simple task. If you think money is a good thing, you can scour the Scriptures and come up with a thousand verses that show the goodness of money and justify your belief. Likewise, if you've made up in your mind that money is evil, there are plenty of verses showing just how evil money can be that will support your theory. Because it is such a significant part of our lives, naturally, the Bible has much to say about our relationship with money. This, however is my favorite: in Ecclesiastes 5:10, the teacher says, "Those who love money will never have enough ..." He continues, "The more you have, the more people come to help you spend it" (v. 11). (Now I see where The Notorious B.I.G. got his inspiration for "Mo' Money, Mo' Problems.") Finally, he states, "What good is wealth—except perhaps to watch it slip through your fingers!" Eight verses later he says this, "it is a good thing to receive wealth from God," and sums it up, "this is indeed a gift from God" (v. 19).

So what's the conclusion? Isn't this a contradiction? In eight short verses how do we get from *What good is wealth?* to *It's a good thing to receive wealth?* It's not a contradiction—it's real life.

This is just one way we can assure that the Bible is relevant; speaking to real life and not fairy tales. I feel like sometimes I go the opposite direction; from verse 19 to verse 11 in just a few short days. Friday morning: *It's payday, my just reward is due for all I've done these past two weeks. How good it is to receive wealth from God!* Sunday night: *This can't be right, all of my automatic drafts hit the same day? Two weeks of work gone in two days of bills and two hours of grocery shopping?* It brings a new meaning to clearing my bank account; the check barely cleared and now everyone else has my money. *What good is wealth, anyway?*

Money is important and money is powerful, but as much as we try to make of it, it's amoral—neither good nor bad. Money is associated with good things: prosperity, wealth, abundance, generosity. These are all terms we read in the Word of God that describe positive financial experiences. But it's also associated with bad things: greed, stinginess, corruption, idolatry. The fact of the matter is that money is just a tool that we use to fulfill our desires.

As an American, the most relevant comparison I can make is with guns. Guns are important to us and they're powerful. A gun can be used to commit a crime or it can be used to stop crime; for sport (target practice, game hunting, and putting food on the table) or for warfare. Simply having or using a gun doesn't speak to value, benefit, wellness, or morality. If you were to ask me if I've ever used my gun and I replied, "I use it every weekend," you could assume I like to hunt or go to the range. But if I clarified and said, "Oh, no, I don't hunt, I rob banks," now you have the information to make an educated value judgment. That's *not* good. Even then, it would be my wicked and twisted heart which holds the desire to do evil and not the gun. How I use it reflects the condition of my heart. Now if you asked the same follow-up question and I said, "No, I'm not a hunter, I'm a police officer, always ready to protect and serve the community," you'd have a different response. We are reminded to honor those working in law enforcement as well as all men and women in uniform, because they walk into danger with courage to keep civilians safe. That *is* good. Again, having a gun in holster alone doesn't spell courage, but the courageous heart discerns when is and isn't the right time to deploy its weapon. This isn't to say a gun plays no role in good or evil; it's a tool—the more powerful it is, the more impact it will have. But how it's used is most certainly the greater determining factor.

Similarly, how we use money reflects our hearts' desires. If you have a problem with money or possessions, I'd like to propose to you that the real problem isn't money, but our desires. We are just using it as a tool. You can't make an accurate judgment call on whether I am good or bad based on how much money I have, and gaining more of it doesn't make me any worse. Then how come we, being the rich, will have such a hard time accepting salvation? Because of our desires. A quick look at your bank statement can indicate how you use money and reveal your desires. Are you satisfied with this life or are you looking forward to God's Kingdom coming to earth with expectation? Have you placed your hope of provision in anything that belongs to you?

> And then he added, "It is what comes from inside that defiles you. For from within, out of a person's heart, come evil thoughts, sexual immorality, theft, murder, adultery, greed, wickedness, deceit, lustful desires, envy, slander, pride, and foolishness. All these vile things come from within; they are what defile you."   (Mark 7:20-23)

That is how Jesus explained it. If this is truly the case, instead of chasing after more money, we should stick to the rivers and the lakes we're planted next to (see Psalm 1:3; see also TLC). Are you equipped for *more*? We ought to look for quality in our hearts before pursuing quantity. Yes, before we set out for greatness, we can anchor our desires in goodness. By examining our hearts, the question shifts from "Is money any good?" to "Is my heart any good?" It gets even more complex than this. For instance, in our hearts, we all have the desire to love. But when our desire to love is misapplied to money, the consequences are "all kinds of evil." This always leads to placing *more* above your morals. So, how can this be redeemed?

The only way to a right heart toward money is the same

way to a right heart toward anything—a right relationship with God. From there, God has direct access to our hearts through His Word and His Holy Spirit. The Holy Spirit uses the process of sanctification to bring results from the spiritual to the natural and make us like Jesus. Our part, as it pertains to our hearts, is our faith, which "shows the reality of what we hope for; it is the evidence of things we cannot see" (Hebrews 11:1). Put simply, we need to trust God for our definition of good and work to ensure that what we believe is right is revealed outwardly in our lives—something we've struggled with since The Garden.

Excuse the *Fresh Prince* reference, but adopting a new perspective on goodness (and greatness) might mean your life gets flipped-turned upside down. It's the reason Jesus came to earth.

In the next half of this book, I plan to "show my work" so you can follow the journey I took to discover God's definition of good as it relates to finances. If you're done with *good* on your own terms, you're in for the best chapter of your life.

8

THIS IS THE BEST CHAPTER

Standouts are going to stand out. It's not about us or money—it's about God.

If this was a book only offering a God-centered approach to finances, I would make this Chapter One, listing scriptures to support my philosophy. If this book was only an inspirational self-help manual, this would be where I share how I came up with my method and the role it played in my rags-to-riches story.

My story is far from being completed; my guess is that I'm in the first half of a rough draft (with emphasis on "rough"). But if I look back, I'm sure I could presume that certain patterns of behavior and thinking have led me to where I am today. I could continue those patterns and get even further along in the future. I could develop a plan for you to replicate and also cite verses that would give my plan credibility.

Okay, that's not entirely true; I couldn't, because when I felt the nudge to write this book, I tried to put that plan together. I quickly discovered that wasn't my assignment for the book. My job was to "show my work." As I peeled back the curtain on my methodology, I learned that it paralleled the journey God already had me on.

When Kerri and I got married, I had this whole finance thing all figured out. First, she moves in; next, we put our money and our debt out on the table; then, we pay off the debt; and finally, we grow wealthy and move to Puerto Rico. I succeeded in getting her to move in. Check. Putting our money on the table was easy, too—we had none. However, I had no idea how much I had underestimated the debt portion. Our table wasn't big enough to park my car, her student loans, or our seven credit cards. Needless to say, this step is where we remained for the next few years. At this rate, we may never get to Puerto Rico.

We set some goals together and despite some initial challenges, we eventually got on the same page and took aim at the great milestone of becoming debt-free. We took a few months to find what our "normal" was—that is, which expenses we should expect each month and how much we spent on average. Then, each month we would pick a category and began setting aside less money to see if we could end the month under-budget. For me, it was a fun game. Kerri, on the other hand, was a lot harder to convince. Being great negotiators, we came to a compromise: whatever you do, there is no way we are touching the hair budget.

This constant cutting forced a change in our own relationship as well as with others, but when we got to cutting restaurant spending, we became infamous. It seemed as though friends and family would invite us to birthday gatherings or organizations where we served would throw lunch meetings at least once a week, and all the while, we settled with being the odd couple who couldn't make it, ate beforehand, or who brought their own food.

Fast forward: a couple years later, I was serving on the curriculum team with Elevate International, a nonprofit dedicated to equipping urban youth and families. During a team meeting, I was asked to write an outline for a class on finances—I guess all our *Will lunch be provided?* requests and *We can't make it; it's not in the budget* replies got their attention. At the time, Kerri and I were on our second trip together through the Bible and I decided I would begin my outline by highlighting every instance in which a verse referenced a financial principle. In just a few books, I could see a common theme developing in this outline: it's not about money, it's about God.

This is what I had already found out as I answered the many (and sometimes highly critical) questions regarding our approach to budgeting. I wasn't standing out because I chose to live according to a budget; I was budgeting because I chose to live as a stand-out. The radical decision to follow Jesus was what set me apart. I knew I was making the right moves, but until that moment, I wasn't showing my work. And as I mentioned earlier, there isn't a simple nugget that I can give you which covers following Jesus wholeheartedly.

So allow me to invite you on the journey I took.

I've compiled a great deal of scriptures, but for this, I'm choosing to use just a few passages along with their contexts because I think they're the most potent and cover practically everything we've discussed up to this point.

THE ONLY SCRIPTURE WE NEED

What better way to start a new journey in walking with God than with prayer? In 1 Chronicles 29:11-18 we find one of my favorite prayers of David:

> "Yours, O Lord, is the greatness, the power, the glory, the victory, and the majesty. Everything in the heavens and on earth is yours, O Lord, and this is your kingdom. We adore you as the one who is over all things. Wealth and honor come from you alone, for you rule over everything. Power and might are in your hand, and at your discretion people are made great and given strength.
>
> "O our God, we thank you and praise your glorious name! But who am I, and who are my people, that we could give anything to you?

> Everything we have has come from you, and we
> give you only what you first gave us! We are here
> for only a moment, visitors and strangers in the land
> as our ancestors were before us. Our days on earth
> are like a passing shadow, gone so soon without a
> trace.
>
> "O Lord our God, even this material we have
> gathered to build a Temple to honor your holy name
> comes from you! It all belongs to you! I know, my
> God, that you examine our hearts and rejoice when
> you find integrity there. You know I have done all
> this with good motives, and I have watched your
> people offer their gifts willingly and joyously.
>
> "O Lord, the God of our ancestors Abraham, Isaac,
> and Israel, make your people always want to obey
> you. See to it that their love for you never changes."
>
> (1 Chronicles 29:11 18)

Thank you, King David! I want to stop right here for a moment to suggest that if your heart isn't on fire right now, you may want to read that passage one more time, or as many times as you need until it lights—we are setting a fire, remember? If we could fully grasp the heart of this prayer, I think we could wrap this book up early. This text doesn't just offer a sound financial perspective, but also a virtuous example of faith in and reverence for God.

Allow me to provide some background for this passage. Earlier in 1 Chronicles, we read that King David had recently recovered the stolen Ark of the Covenant (the seat in the tabernacle reserved for God's presence). As David was settling down in his new home, he had an epiphany. "I am living in a beautiful cedar palace, but the Ark of the Lord's Covenant is out there under a tent!" (1 Chronicles 17:1). For generations, the people of Israel had been setting up the tabernacle as the centerpiece of their camp, according to the procedures God gave Moses in Exodus. It was made to be portable, so they could meet with the Lord on the go. But things had changed since then; they were no longer wandering in the wilderness, no longer fighting for the Promised Land. The king had a permanent home built in Jerusalem; why not the Lord?

As King David shared with the prophet Nathan his intentions, Nathan's initial reply was, "Do whatever you have in mind, for God is with you" (v. 2). But just as it so often happens to us, the plan changed once Nathan heard from the Lord that night. Turns out, even though David had a good motive, God chose to reject his offer to build Him a house, and yet, in a surprising turn of events, God made a covenant promise to David—that He would instead build the house of David (see vv. 8-14). This house would include the short-term promise that a son from David's line would take the throne and that he would be the one to build the Temple for the Lord. There was also the long-term promise that God would make an everlasting kingdom out of David's line, even calling one of these special kings His own Son. (Spoiler alert.)

If David only knew. God essentially told him, "Thank you, but no thank you." David had plans to build God a home, not knowing that God had already made a down payment with His Son. God lived among His people in a temporary structure but David's noble desire unlocked the eternal plan God had all along. Looking back, we believers today have the benefit of knowing the Father as our Creator, Jesus the Son who redeemed us, and the Holy Spirit who dwells within us, making our very bodies a temple (see 1 Corinthians 6:19). But God chose to use David's line to reveal His Son, just as He promised.

> *David had plans to build God a home, not knowing that God had already made a down payment with His Son.*

David was ecstatic about this word from God, but he certainly wasn't complacent about the task of building the Lord's Temple being taken off his plate. I imagine King David routinely asking God about this future Temple, and it seems God revealed more of His plan as the years went by, little by little. In Chapter 22, David is eager to get working on this Temple he is *totally not* building. (I mean, God never said he couldn't gather supplies.) David explains to his son Solomon that God showed him he was the one who would ultimately complete the Temple of the Lord. He makes nearly every preparation possible and offers Solomon some encouragement.

This is where it gets fun. Now, the king is much older and prepared to pass the torch, so he appoints the "young and in-experienced" Solomon as king and addresses all the leaders in Israel about the coming changes. It may be that he just wanted to play as much of a role in building the Temple as possible, or that he knew Solomon would need all the help he could get to pull this thing off, but David surely took the lead. He had already collected "nearly 4,000 tons of gold, 40,000 tons of silver, and so much iron and bronze that it cannot be weighed" (see 1 Chronicles 22:14) as building materials for the Temple. This time, David states,

> "And now, because of my devotion to the Temple of my God, I am giving all of my own private treasures of gold and silver to help in the construction. This is in addition to the building materials I have already collected for his holy Temple. I am donating more than 112 tons of gold from Ophir and 262 tons of refined silver to be used for overlaying the walls of the buildings and for the other gold and silver work to be done by the craftsmen. Now then, who will follow my example and give offerings to the Lord today?"
>
> (1 Chronicles 29:3-5)

Just like that, King David took up an impromptu offering. Can you imagine the scene? I don't know what a ton of gold looks like, though I might use that as a hyperbole to describe Mr. T's dressing room. In this case, we're talking thousands of tons of stone, tons of timber, tons of gold, silver, bronze, iron, and precious stones—tons of tons. *This Temple thing is really gonna happen!*

The leaders who were present saw it, believed, and got excited, too, bringing their even more tons upon tons of materials and money. At the sight of it, they all praised God, including King David, full of joy. *We believed for something good and now God is turning it into something great.*

This is where we come to David's prayer of praise. As I break down the gems embedded in these verses, notice how many of the terms we covered are listed in this one prayer, and how even those not listed are implicitly referenced.

THE SOURCE

First things first: God is our source. At the risk of sounding like he was accepting his first Grammy Award, David clearly recognizes that none of this would be possible without God. He declares that God is in charge of "everything in the heavens and on earth" and affirms, "this is your kingdom." Because it belongs to Him and He is "over all things," God is owed credit for all "the greatness, the power, the glory, the victory, and the majesty" (v. 11). I count at least five times that David gives tribute to where these good gifts came from.

From the time of Abraham in Moriah (see Genesis 22), God had been revealed as the one who provides the best gifts. James says it this way, "Whatever is good and perfect is a gift coming down to us from God our Father, who created all the lights in the heavens" (James 1:17). John the Baptist got it, too, when he stated, "No one can receive anything unless God gives it from heaven." He was speaking of the ministry of Jesus overshadowing his own (see John 3:26-30).

In Psalm 87:7 ESV, the psalmist writes that the people of God would dance and sing "All my springs are in you." (I'm sure it was a hit record.) But I love this picture because a spring is frequently used metaphorically as an unending source of something, and out of a spring flow valuable resources for life in the midst of a desert. And even though we know we can go to any faucet and get water, it would be foolish of us to run to the hardware store and buy a faucet when we get thirsty. A faucet detached from its source is of no value. Do you believe that God "will supply all your needs from his glorious riches?" (Philippians 4:19).

THE OWNER

The second point is related to the first: everything belongs to Him. Yes, everything. David rightly saw that everything *came from* God, but it also *belonged to* Him. He saw God as owner, repeating the word "yours" and saying "your kingdom" and "your people." If he were to receive anything, it would be God's to give. David also saw God as responsible; wealth, honor, power, might, and even the greatness of men, he said, was subject to God's rule.

David writes in Psalm 24:1, "The earth is the Lord's, and everything in it. The world and all its people belong to him." It's all His! And it doesn't stop there: "Look, the highest heavens and the earth and everything in it all belong to the Lord your God" (Deuteronomy 10:14). If everything in the heavens and the earth belong to God, then even the things we call "our own" are rented.

Our very own "possessions" are really not our own at all. In the beginning, everything belonged to Him. Yes that was then, but what about our cell phones and Teslas? Even with modern technology, there is nothing that exists now that didn't start from something God created. Paul writes in Colossians 1:16, "Everything was created through him and for him." (Also see 1 Corinthians 8:6.) By God, through God, and for God. And since David notes that "our days on earth are ... gone so soon" (v. 15), we can be sure that everything we have will return to God after we're long gone.

THE GIVER

The third takeaway is this: God is the reason we have anything to offer. King David testified of the Lord's great grace by acknowledging that the God who created everything by Himself, through Himself, and for Himself didn't keep it all *to* Himself. So every opportunity where we are allowed to participate in "ownership" is a high honor. It is by God's grace alone that we get to "have" anything and being able to give it, therefore, is an even greater blessing.

Yes, everything we have is an invitation to join with God, but because it's all His, there's nothing we have that can add value to Him or increase His quality. In His challenge to Job, God asks this: "Who has given me anything that I need to pay back? Everything under heaven is mine" (Job 41:11). If that wasn't snappy enough, God is recorded addressing His people in Psalm 50 concerning their half-hearted sacrifices by saying, "If I were hungry, I would not tell you, for all the world is mine and everything in it" (Psalm 50:12). God is the owner of "all the animals of the forest" and "the cattle on a thousand hills" (Psalm 50:9-10) so we're not needed in this equation. Even still, God is displeased, not by what we choose to give Him, but by what we *refuse* to give Him.

The glimmer of hope comes at the end of that psalm; there is something we can give to God that will settle our accounts— our gratitude. "But giving thanks is a sacrifice that truly honors me" (Psalm 50:23). This is something David alludes to near the end of his prayer, saying that God rejoices when He finds integrity (or sincerity, stability, and goodness) in our hearts. Aside from that, what else do we have that belongs to us? It's all we have. By offering our thanks from a sincere heart, we fulfill our calling to give God honor with all we have.

THE DIFFERENCE

Realizing that God has no needs, David asks, "who am I, and who are my people ...?" (v. 14). It's a reasonable next question: if we are merely human with nothing to offer, what is it about us He sees that's worth having a relationship? Yet He chose us in Genesis 1 to have a specific role in reflecting His likeness and the specific assignment of having dominion over the earth and everything in it. So anytime we are empowered to bring something to the table, God is the catalyst, and we ought to see it as an invitation to give Him great praise.

I would encourage you to go back and read that prayer all the way through at least once more and allow what flowed from the abundance of David's heart to sink into yours. God didn't have to choose us—He didn't have to choose *anyone*. But not only did He do just that, He actually *wanted to* and still does today. If this doesn't have you overflowing with gratitude, perhaps it's because you already believe you're special. Well, you're right. You *are* special. I just hope you know your uniqueness is not your *doing*; it's your *calling*.

Being called by God to manage what belongs to Him is an honor we're neither worthy to receive nor equipped to carry out—without His involvement, of course. As a follower of Christ, you are different and He is the Difference. We get our playbook from Christ Jesus, following the example of His life and ministry, and we get the cheat code, drawing power from His Holy Spirit. This holy synergy comes with a promise directly from our Lord.

> Remain in me, and I will remain in you. For a branch cannot produce fruit if it is severed from the vine, and you cannot be fruitful unless you remain in me.
> Yes, I am the vine; you are the branches. Those who remain in me, and I in them, will produce much fruit. For apart from me you can do nothing. When you produce much fruit, you are my true disciples. This brings great glory to my Father. (John 15:4-5,8)

This would be a great time to commit to remaining "in Christ" throughout your journey. I believe if you remain connected to Him, you will be made fruitful and the status of all your life will improve, including your financial status. But regardless of what happens for you financially, can you commit to relying on Jesus to be your difference-maker?

Your uniqueness is not your doing; it's your calling.

Do you recognize God as the One who makes all things possible, the One to whom all things belong, and the One from whom all things are given? That's what I extract from this prayer of David; though there is much more to uncover, we must go on. I like to summarize the heart of King David in this prayer this way:

> In our lives, God gets first dibs and He has the final say. It's our privilege to give back to Him everything in between.

A life poured out in this way can be anything but ordinary. We must do the jeopardizing work of taking constant inventory of our hearts and laying them down at His feet. You will receive criticism—like my wife and I did when we began to live according to our strict budget—the most common being, "It doesn't take all that." Duh. We already covered that. This is an opportune time for you to show your work. Who is God to you? What has He done for you and what is your response? Who has He designed you to be and how is He leading you there? The manifestation of the outrageous nature of your calling is evidence that walking with God has set you apart.

It's not about money; it's about God.

As God has invited you to join with Him in the art of ruling and reigning, you have the task of temporarily managing what He has given you. This management concept is what we classically know as *stewardship*. The word has, unfortunately, been misused at times by the Church and even if you don't see it as entirely archaic, it usually leaves a bad taste in your mouth. *Stewardship* is a common euphemism for a local church's never-ending building fund, an arm-twisting giving campaign, or a month-long teaching series meant to encourage congregations to pay their "full tithe." It won't be long before you'll hear, "Will a man rob God?" (see Malachi 3:8).

I've thought about ways that I could turn *stewardship* into an acronym or utilize a clever play on words. I've considered avoiding the word altogether—there are modern ways to explain the concept without having to resort to antiquity. But I'm not going to do it; I'm not going to sugarcoat or shy away from stewardship.

I could say that stewardship means: Showing Thankfulness, Especially With Any Resources Delegated, Serving His Imaginative Purpose. *Hmm, I like that.* Or what if I referred to stewardship as *stewed worship*? *Nah.* It might be helpful to illustrate your participation in God's creation as administration or management. Or in this case, since it's for the Most High: *upper management*? (Oh, I'm definitely going to use that.)

Perhaps we could use more clarification on stewardship than an acronym can provide and maybe the word has more relevance than new slang can give it. There just so happens to be one book that can unlock both these doors. (That's really flattering for you to think, but I'm not talking about *this* book.) As we continue our journey, we'll explore what else the Word has to say on the topic of stewardship.

Are you ready for upper management?

9

PREPARING FOR UPPER MANAGEMENT

The only credit in the Kingdom is faith credited as righteousness.

By now you should be feeling two things: the privilege in the journey that God has you on and the weight of responsibility of that privilege. Getting things right financially hinges on you getting the principle of stewardship, but proper alignment on this topic will consume you to the core. I've shared stories with you along the way in hopes that the concepts which surround stewardship will not only stick with you, but also leave room for you to apply them to your life. As much as I'd like to just define *stewardship* for you, an illustration is far more effective.

Jesus was the best teacher to use this method. He used parables in many of the discussions He had with His followers.

> In fact, in his public ministry he never taught without using parables; but afterward, when he was alone with his disciples, he explained everything to them. (Mark 4:34)

In Matthew 13, the question came up, "Why do you speak to them in parables?" (v. 10). Jesus had just taught in front of a large gathering on the beach, which was usually mixed company made up of those following Jesus, others being discipled by Jesus, and some who outright rejected Jesus. Of course, He instructs them with a parable, as per tradition. Then, He takes His disciples aside—the ones who had committed to have the expression of their lives reflect Jesus's teaching—and addresses why He used parables.

> And he answered them, "To you it has been given to know the secrets of the kingdom of heaven, but to them it has not been given. For to the one who has, more will be given, and he will have an abundance, but from the one who has not, even what he has will be taken away. This is why I speak to them in parables, because seeing they do not see, and hearing they do not hear, nor do they understand."   (Matthew 13:11-13 ESV)

What's great about this explanation is that Jesus was intentional about His style. After He told the stories, He would get away with His disciples and explain the meanings only to them, because those who would reject His message were not permitted by God to understand. Essentially, Jesus saw that without deeper study, parables would be heard as just another story and therefore would shroud unbelievers' minds in a way that would protect them from rejecting the message of Jesus any further. Did you also realize He pretty much responded to their question about parables with another parable?

Clever.

Anyone who can use parables in this way deserves a deeper look and as His followers, we are permitted to receive understanding from these parables. The good news is that we have many records of stories Jesus told, and while about a quarter of them have financial themes, over half of them have some form of principle which we can use to grow in our financial walk. One particular parable stands out among the others, however, and emphasizes the Bible's stance on stewardship.

PUTTING THE 'ABLE' IN PARABLE

In Matthew 25:14-30, Jesus shares a parable sometimes called *The Parable of the Three Servants* and other times known as *The Parable of the Talents*. If you have spent any amount of time in Western church culture, you've most likely heard this story several times before. Jesus uses this parable to illustrate what good stewardship looks like. If it's good enough for Jesus, it's good enough for us. I encourage you to read it in full first; we'll extract some nuggets as we go along.

"Again, the Kingdom of Heaven can be illustrated by the story of a man going on a long trip. He called together his servants and entrusted his money to them while he was gone. He gave five bags of silver to one, two bags of silver to another, and one bag of silver to the last—dividing it in proportion to their abilities. He then left on his trip.

"The servant who received the five bags of silver began to invest the money and earned five more. The servant with two bags of silver also went to work and earned two more. But the servant who received the one bag of silver dug a hole in the ground and hid the master's money.

"After a long time their master returned from his trip and called them to give an account of how they had used his money. The servant to whom he had entrusted the five bags of silver came forward with five more and said, 'Master, you gave me five bags of silver to invest, and I have earned five more.'

"The master was full of praise. 'Well done, my good and faithful servant. You have been faithful in handling this small amount, so now I will give you many more responsibilities. Let's celebrate together!'

"The servant who had received the two bags of silver came forward and said, 'Master, you gave me two bags of silver to invest, and I have earned two more.'

"The master said, 'Well done, my good and faithful servant. You have been faithful in handling

> this small amount, so now I will give you many more responsibilities. Let's celebrate together!'
>
> "Then the servant with the one bag of silver came and said, 'Master, I knew you were a harsh man, harvesting crops you didn't plant and gathering crops you didn't cultivate. I was afraid I would lose your money, so I hid it in the earth. Look, here is your money back.'
>
> "But the master replied, 'You wicked and lazy servant! If you knew I harvested crops I didn't plant and gathered crops I didn't cultivate, why didn't you deposit my money in the bank? At least I could have gotten some interest on it.'
>
> "Then he ordered, 'Take the money from this servant, and give it to the one with the ten bags of silver. To those who use well what they are given, even more will be given, and they will have an abundance. But from those who do nothing, even what little they have will be taken away. Now throw this useless servant into outer darkness, where there will be weeping and gnashing of teeth.'"
>
> (Matthew 25:14-30)

At face value, it's a pretty well-fashioned story. It has the rhythm of those classic moral fables they used to read to us when we were kids. They always ended with a sweet takeaway in the form of a one-liner followed by something bizarre, and this is no different—thanks to the whole "weeping and gnashing of teeth" part. Anyway, let's get into the meat, one chunk at a time:

> "Again, the Kingdom of Heaven can be illustrated by the story of a man going on a long trip. He called together his servants and entrusted his money to them while he was gone. He gave five bags of silver to one, two bags of silver to another, and one bag of silver to the last—dividing it in proportion to their abilities. He then left on his trip."   (vv. 14-15)

We start the story right off the bat with a man who sounds quite wealthy in his own right. My first indication of this is that

I'm not much of a "long trip" kind of guy. What do you consider to be a "long trip?" I have a feeling this guy didn't spend any time calculating how much PTO he accumulated while he was planning this getaway. He didn't click that "flexible dates" button on the flight finder and play that all-too-familiar game of broke-airfare bingo, trying to decide which flights on which days would provide the cheapest trip. *Aha! If I leave on Tuesday and come back the same Tuesday, I can save twelve bucks. But if I leave Thursday, I could come back three Fridays from now and save the most money. Hopefully, by then I'll be able to find a steady job out there with some PTO, because I won't have one to come back to.* I'm guessing he didn't do that.

But it's what he did do that tells even more. He called together his servants—*oh, right, he has servants.* I'm pretty sure we're not talking about calling to place a hold on the house-cleaning service he found on Groupon. He had actual servants working for him. Before going on this trip, he reaches out to these fellows and has a board meeting with them. Well, that's odd. I've never been a servant by profession, but even as an employee, I haven't gotten any invites from the CEO to a meeting like this. During the meeting, he starts divvying up their shares of his money to them. Okay, I'll say it: there's something very strange about this man. I've never been in charge of servants, but I feel like this is breaking some kind of code from *Being a Master 101: How To Keep It All To Yourself.* If you want to see it again, you don't entrust your own money to your own servants.

Finally, I believe it's important to note how the servants received their portions. The man saw it best to diversify his assets and temporarily place them in the hands of these servants. In this illustration, all three servants were given something to manage, but they were given different amounts. The master could have used any system to split the pot (my favorite is rock-paper-scissors). Being six-foot-five, I also wouldn't object to him lining them up tallest to shortest. But instead of using chance or something physical and material, the master looked elsewhere. He knew his servants well enough to evaluate them based on internal attributes, which I don't know how to do. My wife has this uncanny ability to put a seemingly random number to anything. I can ask her how hungry she is and she will give me some number like 64.5 out of 100. *What scale were you using to quantify that?* Though she *is* able to justify it, much like in this parable, she doesn't share her method of instant calculation. So what was the distinguishing factor? The amounts were distributed proportionately according to each of the servants' abilities.

Ability is key.

GOOD PORTION

Have you considered your ability the last time you were praying for increase? It's one thing for us to acknowledge that everything we have is given to us by God, but in the same thought, we often complain about our dissatisfaction with the amount we've received. Your portion is directly correlated to your ability.

If you have a problem with your portion, you may want to take a look at your ability.

This leads me to ask the question: ability for what? Everyone brings to the table different skills and abilities in life and it would reveal quite an imperfect system to look at just one category to make this type of judgment call. What was the man looking for in his servants? While the methodology isn't revealed during the distribution, it is made clearer as we read further.

> "The servant who received the five bags of silver began to invest the money and earned five more. The servant with two bags of silver also went to work and earned two more. But the servant who received the one bag of silver dug a hole in the ground and hid the master's money.
>
> After a long time their master returned from his trip and called them to give an account of how they had used his money. The servant to whom he had entrusted the five bags of silver came forward with five more and said, 'Master, you gave me five bags of silver to invest, and I have earned five more.'

> The master was full of praise. 'Well done, my good and faithful servant. You have been faithful in handling this small amount, so now I will give you many more responsibilities. Let's celebrate together!' The servant who had received the two bags of silver came forward and said, 'Master, you gave me two bags of silver to invest, and I have earned two more.'
>
> The master said, 'Well done, my good and faithful servant. You have been faithful in handling this small amount, so now I will give you many more responsibilities. Let's celebrate together!'" (vv. 16-23)

To sum it up, the first two servants pleased their master by investing the money and doubling it. By this, they demonstrated the ability which determined how the money was apportioned. When he gave them a performance review, the master revealed what he initially saw in his servants. First, he praised these guys for a job "well done" and called them "good." But what did they do? They took what he gave them and turned it into more. So is this a case where *more* means *gooder*? Could it be that the man, like us, sees greatness and calls it good? There's way more to it than that. He describes their actions as "faithful" but calls what they were managing a "small amount." And in return, he offers them more responsibilities.

This master knew his servants and their abilities well. But until they put that ability to work, it was unseen and untested. From this, we can derive the definition of *faithfulness*. Faithfulness is how you demonstrate your ability. Like a sponge, what's in us comes out when we are under pressure. Can I count on you to outwardly work an internal ability that I believe you possess? That's faithfulness. Remember, faith is evidence of the unseen (see Hebrews 11:1). Well then, the same goes with faithfulness. How evident is it that you have the capacity to handle life's common challenges?

These two servants quickly found out the secret of faithfulness: with faithfulness comes opportunity. They started out with some bags of money (remember my warning of baglytransported money). But after their review, there's no telling what they were in charge of. The master basically says, "Because you were faithful, you will receive more responsibilities." And not just more but "many more." So let's get this straight: you start with what you are given—*some*; you put it to work and make *more*; the master sees the bigger picture and calls it *small*; and then he endows you with *much more*. That's the resource paradox at work.

I can't cover this excerpt without addressing that last line of the master's speech. The master threw a party for each of the first two servants. There is something about demonstrating your ability that is worth celebrating.

RAW TALENT

Before he divided the resources, the master believed he could trust each servant with the amount he gave to them. He believed in their ability to manage their "small amount." And for the first two servants, the faith the man placed in them was validated by their faithfulness.

Because this parable is often called *The Parable of the Talents* in other translations, there is an unfortunate word confusion present. In this case, a *talent* is an old unit of measurement used to weigh money—hence the NLT translating it "bags of silver." Couple that with the master's decision to divide according to their "abilities," and this parable is often mistaken to be teaching about your God-given talents and what you do with them. This idea really limits the point of the story.

When you equate the "talent" of the recipients with the "talents" (money) they were given, it makes it easy to believe there isn't much we can do about what we've been given. The lesson starts at what you received—did you get five, two, or one? When we do this, we miss the importance of the chief talent mentioned in the verse prior. The key to unlocking the meaning of this parable is what comes *before* the distribution.

God *did* give you the privilege and the ability to manage everything He's given you. So, sure, your raw talent and giftedness is a part of the equation, but it's stewardship in general— this overarching ability to manage—that trumps other abilities. That's the main lesson being taught.

The beauty here is that ability to manage can be developed, which means the key that unlocks this whole concept is not something outside your control. Since we're talking about upper management in this case, let's talk about how you can increase your ability to manage money.

> ### *If you don't choose where you want your money to go, chances are, it will just go.*

BUDGET.

That's not a noun; it's a verb. Do it. You should budget. You have a Why List, which is a physical (or digital) expression of your priorities and values. You probably keep a calendar, planner, or to-do list. Your calendar expresses your priorities and values in relation to the resource of time. Your budget expresses them through money. When you budget, you are breaking down the money you have into categories of items you expect to pay. The goal is to get ahead of your spending so you can decide where it goes before it's gone.

Think about it this way: everything you make will eventually be spent. The spending will either happen by chance or it will happen by choice. Just like with time, if you don't choose where you want your money to go, chances are, it will just go. I am suggesting that *you* choose how you spend your money—down to the last dime. This doesn't mean squandering what you have on retail purchases but considering present needs, future obligations, today's luxuries, and tomorrow's dreams, and paying yourself until they become due.

This usually starts with **tracking**. This is where you take a month or so to enter each transaction as you make a purchase in order to find a baseline. You then organize these transactions into categories and categories into groups, for example: Gas, Groceries, Clothing, and Entertainment might be separate categories in the Everyday Expenses group. You might group your bill categories like Mortgage/Rent, Water, Electricity, Internet, and Phone. You should have an idea of when you will make the next transaction for all of these.

When you move on to **delegating**, you look ahead for a short time (usually the next month) and allocate the money that flows into your account to your categories as needed. Sure, you may get a check for $500, but that doesn't mean you have $500—you have next week's groceries and half of next month's rent. The game plan for delegation is to fund the categories using only money you actually have in the bank. This way, you can begin to make purchases based on money that is available in each category rather than what's available in your account.

Tracking and *delegating* become habitual over time. The more you get paid and the more often, the more you will have to delegate. The more you spend, the more you will have to track. Next, you will begin **evaluating** the performance of the categories. When you notice that paying down debt is exhilarating, for example, you might search other areas you can cut back in order to intensify your efforts. From time to time, unexpected expenses will come up that you haven't properly funded. When this happens, you simply take money from one or more of the other categories to balance them out. If unexpected charges become a regular occurrence, it's time to start expecting them. You can delegate additional money or change whatever behavior you need to eliminate that expense.

If *evaluating* is where you look down the road for impending charges, **reserving** is where you zoom out to the aerial view. These items may not come up for months, years, or decades, but you can still assign your money to these categories knowing you'll need them in the future. Any money that's left after you've delegated them to all your bills and basic needs is not *extra* money. By placing these in a reserve category, you are effectively saying, "No, I will not eat this money or pour it into my gas tank." You'll reserve for things such as your kids' education, your retirement, home and vehicle repairs and upgrades, new phones and computers, even the funds you need to start that business. Since this money is spoken for, the categories to which these items belong should reveal where you're headed.

Considering the parable, step into the shoes of the master for a moment. (Is that too presumptuous?) We love to look through the eyes of the servants whenever we talk about this passage—and we'll spend the next few chapters doing just that—but at least when it comes to our bank accounts, we're a lot more like the master. Humor me, okay?

The master was in charge of servants. You are in charge of your money, which is meant to fulfill every financial need that will arise in the near or distant future. And it's not just one servant, every category you fund becomes another servant at your disposal. As a master, knowing your online banking password or your account balance isn't enough—to truly become a master of your money, you've got to tell it what to do. So, you budget.

The master in the parable was budgeting, too. He delegated his money based on the tracking he had done. After a while, he evaluated his servants' performance and added to ones who performed well while taking away from the one who did not. Here is an easy assessment: credit cards are lousy servants. They may fool you into believing their convenience or reward points are serving you but they aren't. These categories are the type which perform poorly yet you'll have to delegate more funds to eliminate them. I recommend the Debt Snowball method which Dave Ramsey details in his book *The Total Money Makeover*.[11]

We also know the master kept reserves. For one, he went on a long trip, and when he came back, he threw a couple of parties. Likewise, you are going to be throwing some parties and taking trips when your categories meet your financial goals.

I write all that to say: you are responsible for far more than you give yourself credit. If, like me, you have felt like a victim of your circumstances, you may not realize how much your efforts influence your financial results. You *can* increase your ability to manage. You are not left to the fate of either servant number one, two, or three based on what cards you were dealt. This isn't simply a case of "the haves and the have nots."

But then again, there *is* that third servant ...

10

THE DIFFERENCE BETWEEN HAVES AND HAVE NOTS

When you know what you have, that's enough to overcome what you don't. — Dr. Michael Maiden

I used to always read *The Parable of the Talents* from a poverty mindset, because it's how I grew up. I won't say that I grew up poor; in fact, when I was still a toddler, my dad landed a job that afforded us the opportunity to move from a neighborhood known for its struggle to one in the suburbs of Phoenix, thriving with potential. This new neighborhood was where all the middle-class families migrated so they could make sure their kids attended the best public schools the city had to offer. That was the story for most of our new neighbors, though it seemed like for everyone else it was more of a lateral move to a better school district. For us, we were *have nots* living in a land of the *haves*.

In a sense, it was a lateral move for our family, too. The streets were safer, the environment was welcoming, the schools performed better, but the standard of living was offset by the cost of living—so other than the home, we didn't see much new "stuff". When you and everyone around you lives in poverty, it seems as if even envy is scarce. You don't really know what you don't have until you see someone else with it. All of a sudden your eyes are opened to the knowledge of good and *are you kidding me, you've got two TVs?!*

My eyes weren't opened until adolescence. Shortly after Christmas, when all the kids of the neighborhood were enjoying the one and a half solid weeks with their new presents, my friends and I went for our usual bike ride. This year, however, two of the guys rolled up sporting the top-of-the-line models of the most prestigious brands in the market. At least, that's what they told me. (How would I know?) They proceeded to let me know just how great their bikes were, with all their features— front and back pegs, lightweight frame, upgraded pedals for extra grip. They were basically riding the Teslas of BMX bikes. They also were gracious enough to let me know how inferior mine was. It was a no-name toy, built like a tank, and sometimes the chain would slip off if I went too fast.

Of course I wouldn't be able to ride as quickly or follow the same trails or do the same tricks as the other guys; I didn't have the right equipment. I mean, it did everything I had wanted it to do the day before, but at that moment, it became junk. My friends had no idea what was going on for me internally; they weren't intentionally trying to make me feel second-rate. Nevertheless, I began to hear the whispers of discontent.

NOT NOTHING

Okay, going back to the parable of the talents. I'd like to get a bit controversial as I discuss the third servant more in depth. As the story continues:

> "Then the servant with the one bag of silver came and said, 'Master, I knew you were a harsh man,

> harvesting crops you didn't plant and gathering crops you didn't cultivate. I was afraid I would lose your money, so I hid it in the earth. Look, here is your money back.'
>
> But the master replied, 'You wicked and lazy servant! If you knew I harvested crops I didn't plant and gathered crops I didn't cultivate, why didn't you deposit my money in the bank? At least I could have gotten some interest on it.' Then he ordered, 'Take the money from this servant, and give it to the one with the ten bags of silver."   (Matthew 25:24-28)

I don't know why, but I feel for the third servant. Because of the above verses, I've always disliked this parable—seriously, it was one of my least favorite passages of the Bible. I've always seen it as confirmation that the rich get richer and the poor get poorer; it's just not fair.

As an advocate for the third servant, I'd like to plead his case. The guy who starts with the least ends up with nothing and the one who already has plenty and doesn't need anything gets a bonus? When you're operating in scarcity, you're clearly closer to losing what you have than those with abundance. Fear, it should follow, is a natural response to lack. The other guys might think this is a fun game—who can bring back the most money?—but that's what a little cushion will do for you. It makes risky situations less ... well, risky. And it makes loss less painful. Apparently, this third servant is so afraid to lose his master's money that he opts out of the game completely. And rightly so. You only have one bag, so this is *not* a game. It makes me think of those commercials from the wealth-management companies. First they disclaim any guarantee, telling you that investing comes with a risk of losing your initial investment, and then they let you know there's a six-figure minimum investment to participate. No, thank you. I'm out.

When was the last time you "opted out"?

It's funny because most of the time I choose to opt out, it's after being rejected or, like in the case of the wealth-management company commercials, not having enough to begin with. But something about this scenario is different.

Did you notice? There are three servants in this story and though the portion they received is related to their abilities, they all get *something*. (Bear with me as I awaken my inner math geek.) The master gives out a total of eight bags of silver, splitting it into bags of five, two, and one. This means one servant got 62.5 percent, another 25 percent and the last got 12.5 percent. Surely I'm speculating here, but this master was quite thorough. I believe if the master thought the third servant had zero ability, he would have received zero money to manage.

Nobody gets nothing.

There's a story of a widow in 2 Kings 4 that really speaks to this truth:

> One day the widow of a member of the group of prophets came to Elisha and cried out, "My husband who served you is dead, and you know how he feared the Lord. But now a creditor has come, threatening to take my two sons as slaves."
>
> "What can I do to help you?" Elisha asked. "Tell me, what do you have in the house?"
>
> "Nothing at all, except a flask of olive oil," she replied.'   (2 Kings 4:1-2)

Nice save! Before Elisha demonstrates provision coming through a miraculous multiplication, he starts with taking inventory of what she has. The widow's immediate response to Elisha's prophetic investigation was "I have nothing." She's asking for help. And when you're in I Need Help Mode, you are vastly more familiar with what you don't have than what you do. Remember, the dichotomy we spoke of earlier between being needy and being privileged? It's easy to be one or the other. Yet the moment she made mention of the one exception to her lack, albeit insignificant, she had more than zero.

If you are in a place right now where you are lacking some of the basics, you don't have to ignore the facts. The fact might be that you are in mounds of debt. The fact might be that you have more rent due than your bank account has funds. The fact might be that you are undereducated for your desired career. The fact might be that you have been handed the short end of the stick. These facts shaped my reality, too. But if that's the rule, what's your exception? Even if you're not in the same boat as me, quietly rooting on the one-talent servant, pause for just a moment and consider what you have going for you.

The verses in the passage that follow outline one of Elisha's many recorded miracles. The widow is instructed to borrow as many empty jars as she can find—she gathers vessels that aren't being used well. She is told to get with her sons (another resource she had going for her) and fill up the jars, pouring from her flask of oil. Her little flask doesn't run out until all the larger vessels are full, and she is able to sell the oil, pay off her debts, and live on the rest. Because she has something to work with and she puts it to use, she goes from bankrupt to retirement in the span of one day.

I don't believe we would have the same account had she stopped at "nothing."

To illustrate my math wizardry even further, go ahead and take zero and multiply it by 1 million. Now do the same thing starting with one. That's extremely simple, right? It's imperative that you have *something*. We're back to the resource paradox, except in this instance, it appears to work by perception. Conversely, neglecting to perceive resources seems to render the concept ineffective.

Scripture says the three servants received "in proportion to their abilities," so this third servant had no excuse. It's not that he had no ability, but that he refused to even demonstrate the little ability he did have. In the game, he was outmatched five-to-one and two-to-one. But this wasn't a game; he received a *real* bag of money. He had *something*. Blinded by a fear of "nothing," he buried it in the earth. He rendered what he had of no use.

As a result, what happened? He lost his opportunity to manage.

OPPORTUNITY COSTS

In my story, once I realized that my bike was trash—next to nothing—I buried it in my garage. Because I was embarrassed, because I didn't want to feel like the lowest man on the totem pole, because I had chosen to opt out, I kept my bike hidden and often exchanged something for nothing. Several times, my friends asked if I wanted to go bike riding—a question to which my normal response would have been "when and where?"—but I quickly declined. Instead of spending time, I chose to save face. I gave up exercise, experience with the bike I had, and the time to bond and grow in relationship with my friends.

If you re-read the story of the servants, you'll notice the third servant lost his opportunity to manage long before the master took it away in Matthew 25:18. He gave up this privilege when he placed the money where it didn't belong. Just as important as recognizing that you have something (as opposed to nothing) is how you use it.

We don't know how long the man went away on vacation, but every hour of his absence was another hour the first two servants were able to make a return on their investment. The money they received was put to work *for* them. Therefore, the master's time away was to their benefit. Conversely, the longer the money sat in a bad investment, the gap of what could have been grew wider and wider.

One of the most important resources of any investment is time. Many different formulas are used to predict the returns you will make following your initial investment, but the element of time is often undervalued and overlooked in those equations. When you decide to put your money at risk, you are usually committing those funds to a process for a season. The longer it remains committed to the process, the greater chance you will see the desired effects of that process. Of course, the more time you leave a resource assigned to one formula is less time that you'll be able to see the potential effects of other options. When faced with many choices about how you'll employ your resources, saying "yes" to one option is essentially saying "no" to every other alternative.

All of this is considered when weighing difficult decisions in business, finance, real estate, and the like. They factor in what is called opportunity cost—the potential gains that must be forfeited when choosing one option over another—to determine if a commitment is worth the risk. The concept of opportunity cost, however, goes well beyond economics. We actually calculate this in our own heads when we decide what to eat or even what we say. That is why we choose our words *and our meals* carefully; every choice leads you down a new road with a different set of possibilities. We also factor in opportunity cost when determining what show we will binge watch on Netflix or where we will live, what company we work for, or who we will spend our life with.

Ladies, let me let you in on a little secret. The moment a man completes his opportunity cost evaluation, he makes a firm decision regarding the fate of your relationship. I'm not saying he's walking around with a checklist and recording voice notes about you—only a person crazy enough to write this book would do that—but there *is* an assessment going on inside his head. (Someone tell Beyoncé it's not as simple as I "like it" so I'll "put a ring on it.") For some, this happens rather quickly and for others, it takes time, but once a guy is convinced that not being with you will leave him worse off than committing his life to you, he's ready to go shopping. And I mean to say this carefully: ladies, you do get to play a part in the convincing process, helping him see committing to you as the only option worth his investment.

(I'm giving you the following gem for free.)

If he can withdraw benefits without the risk of forfeiting other options, he probably will.

It's natural for us to choose an option with the lowest opportunity cost, but it's not always that easy. On the one hand, making a decision impulsively and without assessing the benefits of other options can be detrimental. It's also easy to get so overwhelmed with choices that you make no decision at all. With so many options available as to how you will spend your time and money and energy, "analysis paralysis" is a common problem we all have to deal with. The trouble with making no decision, is that "nothing" *is* a decision.

Choosing nothing is always the decision with the highest cost. It's the logic behind the famous poem by William F. O'Brien, "Better to Try and Fail Than Never to Try at All". There is actually some value in taking the risk that often goes unseen—memories, experience, and confidence all added to your account regardless of the outcome. The master told the third servant he would have been satisfied with some measly bank interest, so it's clear the goal wasn't spectacular. He didn't require that his servants bring back double.

FEAR FACTOR

By choosing not to put the money in the bank, this guy gave up something for nothing. He's not alone. When we weigh our options, sometimes with a **finite eyesight**, we make inaccurate calculations by not seeing what we have. Sometimes we get hit with **analysis paralysis**. Sometimes we look at our peers and suffer **comparison embarrassment**. In all of these examples, what we're battling is really a false belief, and that's where we choose to opt out.

The third servant had ability, money, and time all functioning as part of the equation when he made his decision. Have you ever had everything you need to pull the trigger on something but still didn't feel right about it? Part of calculating the cost is feeling good about your choice, and this poor man was riddled with fear. You can't say he made *that* bad of a decision, considering the cost. Fear can cost us everything we have fought for. In the book of Joshua, Rahab spills the beans that everyone in the city is afraid of the Israelites. We later learn that Jericho's walls were slammed shut so they could prolong what they knew was going to happen (see Joshua 2:9; 6:1).

If I were to tell you that your Heavenly Father has found you worthy of managing millions of dollars worth of resources on His behalf, would that delight you or lead you to run for cover? That's the reality you're living in right now. He believes you possess the ability to take those resources and put them to use. Do you believe what He believes about you?

If that idea freaks you out, I get it. It's a huge responsibility and what evidence is there to prove that God isn't making a terrible mistake by choosing to use us? That's easy. *You* provide the evidence. (*Chris, you're not helping!*) God has provided substantial evidence throughout creation and its history that He is all-powerful and all-knowing. We can be sure He didn't get this one wrong. Being faithful means we believe about ourselves what God does and we work out this belief. We need not be worried about losing for His sake. Let's be clear, what does He have to lose? The focus is not on the results, but on the belief—or faith. That's where the reward comes in. And as we read on, we see it gets even less complicated:

> "To those who use well what they are given, even more will be given, and they will have an abundance. But from those who do nothing, even what little they have will be taken away."   (v. 29)

I love comparing thought-for-thought translations like the NLT with word-for-word translations like the ESV and in this instance, I feel like the NLT is giving us the whole Bible study before we even dive in! The ESV (along with many common word-for-word translations) says it this way:

> "For to everyone who has will more be given, and he will have an abundance. But from the one who has not, even what he has will be taken away."
>   (Matthew 25:29 ESV)

We're back to the "haves" and "have nots." The currency flows "to everyone who has" and "from the one who has not." Not surprising. The question is: has what? Well, what distinguishes them? Their social status? Their abilities? Their method? Their results? It was **faithfulness**—demonstrated belief under authority—that separated the two from the one.

Just as the world has taught us, Jesus says there are two types of people: the "haves" and the "have nots." But there's hope in this kind, because a *have not* can become a *have* by way of faithfulness. Did you see how this was rendered in the NLT? The two types of people in this world are not the *haves* and the *have nots*, but the "use wells" and the "do nothings." We are either using well what we have or we are doing nothing. This goes beyond just giving more to those who have. When we demonstrate the ability we have to manage what was entrusted to us (faithfulness), we will receive more opportunities to manage. The same is true in reverse—opportunities are lost when we refuse to demonstrate our ability.

> *Abundance is not a result of what you have or what you've been given. It's the result of how you manage.*

I want you to notice how much of the master's final declaration in verse 29 was his judgment, and how much was him stating the facts. Even before taking the money from the third servant to give to the one with ten, the first two servants had already received "more responsibilities." And even before that, they had both doubled what they started with. They simply received more of what was to come on the path they were already following. The servant who had started with two bags, didn't even get a share in the third servant's forfeited loot. But verse 29 is just as true for him as it was for the first guy, just as the statement passes muster for the third servant regardless of his portion being given away. He just received an acceleration of what was to come on the path he chose. Eventually, the third servant would have lost his right to manage and had nothing to show for it.

And let us not gloss over that wealth promise: the *use wells* "will have an abundance." If we continue down the path of faithfulness, we will be rewarded with more and more opportunities. Included in these opportunities will be times where we get to experience abundance. Abundance is not a result of what you have or what you've been given. It's the result of how you manage. Are you a *use well* believer?

I shall digress about the disparities between the *haves* and the *have nots*, but I'm not done with that third servant. Let's get serious here, the master was a "harsh man" (v. 24), he didn't say when he'd be back, and it's not like he gave them specific instructions on what to do with the money. The third servant tried to avoid putting someone else's money at risk of loss. Wouldn't that be the smartest choice of all? How can we determine what's the right move? The game-changer lies in the distinction between wisdom and foolishness, which is what we'll discuss in the next chapter. It looks something like this:

Use Well: Wisdom
Do Nothing: Foolishness

11

A WORD TO THE WISE

We grieve the Holy Spirit when we do things He doesn't want us to do. We quench the Spirit when we don't do the things He wants us to do.

If we are to fully understand stewardship, it would make sense that we want to be wise. Considering that—if I may blame it on Jesus—He just narrowed everyone down to the *use wells* and the *do nothings* and assigned to them wisdom and foolishness, respectively, we have to address the concept of wisdom further. We'll get back to the three servants later. First, here are some random words of wisdom.

- "No journey is too great when one finds what he seeks."
- "You win some, you lose some. But you live, you live to fight another day."
- "Make the money, don't let the money

make you."
- "The beauty of contentment is there are no qualifications."

That last one is my own.

I have an awkward confession. When I was in seventh grade, I started my career as a philosopher and dating consultant. I used to make my own words of wisdom—like the ones above—and then I'd eavesdrop on any and every conversation until I found the perfect opportunity to exhibit my profundity. My classmates began to come to me for answers to life's toughest questions—answers which quickly resembled less Dr. Phil and more Chinese Buffet fortune cookie. Soon after, the inevitable happened—I received my first request for dating advice.

This was several years before the movie *Hitch*, but our approaches were surprisingly similar. I came up with a wise strategy to allow my friend to capture the attention of his love interest. During our recess football game, I was going to run a wide passing route in the direction of a group of jump-roping girls. He would arrive on the scene a hero from the sidelines, pushing me out of the way and catching the ball, saving the ladies in the process. After tossing the ball my way, he was free to introduce himself and close the deal (whatever we thought that meant).

Everything went according to plan—the execution was sloppy, sure, and I don't think he caught the ball, either. The whole thing actually looked pretty obvious, but it didn't appear that the jump-rope gang suspected a thing. And as fate would have it, he got the girl. They dated for a few weeks—enough time to be named "Cutest Couple" in the school yearbook. At that point, even I was surprised at my success, but there was no stopping me. Despite the fact that none of my fellow classmates ever saw me date someone at school, a number of them came to me to be matched or to stage a set-up.

You see, the truth is, I knew just enough to be dangerous. I didn't have the guts to ask anyone out myself—that's way too much of a commitment—but I would gladly and vicariously encourage you to the life I hoped for. I learned then what I'm learning now while writing this book: wisdom is far easier said than done.

It's common for us to see wisdom as synonymous with smarts—brains, intelligence, intellect. Foolishness is just the opposite, akin to ignorance—stupid, dumb, ridiculous. In the Bible, that only scratches the surface. In reality, wisdom is more than mental; it's moral. You can be smart and lack wisdom because biblical wisdom is not found in the head, but the heart.

In the Old Testament, the Hebrew word for wisdom is *khokhmah*. (If you pronounced it correctly, feel free to spit that one out now.) In Exodus 31, one of my favorite folks in the Bible gets an early glimpse of this wisdom. As verse 3 puts it, Bezalel is said to be filled with the Spirit of God (yes, that's the Holy Spirit—the same Spirit that we New Testament followers of Jesus get to experience within us daily), which afforded him "great wisdom, ability, and expertise in all kinds of crafts." He ends up being appointed lead designer of the tabernacle and everything in it; working with jewels and precious metals, wood and fabric, and more, to accomplish this awesome God-ordained task.

> The Lord has filled Bezalel with the Spirit of God, giving him great wisdom, ability, and expertise in all kinds of crafts. He is a master craftsman, expert in working with gold, silver, and bronze. He is skilled in engraving and mounting gemstones and in carving wood. He is a master at every craft. And the Lord has given both him and Oholiab son of Ahisamach, of the tribe of Dan, the ability to teach their skills to others. The Lord has given them special skills as engravers, designers, embroiderers in blue, purple, and scarlet thread on fine linen cloth, and weavers. They excel as craftsmen and as designers.
>
> (Exodus 35:31-35)

It doesn't say whether he instantly became a "master in every craft" or if he already had mad skills as an interior decorator, but that doesn't matter, since everything he had was first given to him by God. In this instance, wisdom was given to Bezalel freely but this privilege came with a purpose. From this we can gather that biblical wisdom is the result of a given skill—or ability—put to work in order to do something good. Which re-raises the question: what is good? Do we get to determine what *good* is? Remember, *greater* doesn't mean *gooder*. Good is a standard solely determined by the Lord.

WHAT DO YOU WANT?

Shortly after David prayed that profound prayer in 1 Chronicles 29—seriously, turn to the next page—his son Solomon was established as king. Following David's death, God appeared to Solomon in a dream and urged him, "What do you want? Ask, and I will give it to you!" (2 Chronicles 1:7).

Before we go on and read this fairly familiar passage, I want to interject a sidebar. Wouldn't it be nice if God came to us and told us to ask for *anything*? Well get a load of this:

> "Ask, and it will be given to you; seek, and you will find; knock, and it will be opened to you."
> (Matthew 7:7)
> "If you abide in Me, and My words abide in you, you will ask what you desire, and it shall be done for you." (John 15:7)
> Now this is the confidence that we have in Him, that if we ask anything according to His will, He hears us. (1 John 5:14)

We have the same promise given to Solomon. And we have the same Spirit given to Bezalel. Jesus also said this about you:

> "I tell you the truth, of all who have ever lived, none is greater than John the Baptist. Yet even the least person in the Kingdom of Heaven is greater than he is!" (Matthew 11:11)

If John the Baptist topped Jesus's list of the greatest men in history at that time, he's above Solomon. And you're a part of the Kingdom, which means you are, too. The point I'm making is this: Solomon isn't extra special—*you* are. I'd say that about levels the playing field. So stop waiting for God to interrupt your dream and just ask for what you want.

Okay, let's move on.

There are two separate accounts of this interaction between God and Solomon and we're going to dive into the record in 1 Kings 3. If your Bible has headers at the top, you'll most likely see that the title of this section is something like, "Solomon Asks for Wisdom." Don't check out because you've heard this story before. Why don't we challenge what we think we know?

> Solomon replied, "You showed great and faithful love to your servant my father, David, because he was honest and true and faithful to you. And you have continued to show this great and faithful love to him today by giving him a son to sit on his throne.
>
> "Now, O Lord my God, you have made me king instead of my father, David, but I am like a little child who doesn't know his way around. And here I am in the midst of your own chosen people, a nation so great and numerous they cannot be counted!"
>
> (1 Kings 3:6-8)

Solomon acknowledged the great responsibility placed on his shoulders, but to him, his portion seemed greater than his ability. He was probably freaking out. He grew up the son of a king, but not the firstborn. Or second or third; he was somewhere closer to tenth in line to the throne, so he wasn't preparing to be king his whole life. He was kicking back and enjoying the finer things in life, so leading millions of people was all brand-new to him. He says, "You have made me king ... but I am like a little child who doesn't know his way around" (v. 7). Basically he said: "I have no idea what I'm doing, I don't know the ropes." And this is just the prelude to his request—my portion to manage is greater than my ability—then he gets to the nitty-gritty. Here's his request:

> "Give me an understanding heart so that I can govern your people well and know the difference

> between right and wrong. For who by himself is able to govern this great people of yours?" (1 Kings 3:9)

In response to God's petition, Solomon asked for the ability to do a good job leading the people. There was a purpose for the skill he was asking for—to apply it to the service he was called to do by God. Solomon didn't just ask for a *what*, he gave the *why*—a *what* and a *for*. Technically speaking, Solomon didn't ask for wisdom as we know it; he asked God to help him be a good steward.

What lesson can we learn from Solomon so far? Firstly, there's **ownership**. One thing Solomon knew well was that his role as king was a stewardship opportunity. When faced with choices, it's important that you know what is your responsibility and own it. Next is **humility**. Solomon may have gone overboard with this one, but even with the title of king, he wasn't afraid to let God know he needed help. God is not surprised when we tell Him, "I have no idea what I'm doing" when our portion is greater than our perceived ability. **Expectation** follows when you believe the God you're asking will actually help you. Solomon's request was to manage "this great people" *well*. If you can believe for goodness, expect God to handle the greatness. Finally, there was **willingness**. Solomon, knowing the giant footsteps he was following in, recognized that he had the best chance of succeeding if he wasn't "by himself." God can do more with a renegade who is interested in knowing His will than with a calculated individualist. Willingness precedes faithfulness.

NONE THE WISER

Thanks to Sunday School, most of us could tell the story from here. This unselfish request of Solomon pleased God, so God granted Solomon great wisdom and, among other things, great riches. He said "I will give you what you asked for" (v. 12), then He continued, "And I will also give you what you did not ask for—riches and fame!" (v. 13). Solomon went on to be one of the wisest men to ever live as well as the most wealthy and the most well-known in his day.

> So the Lord gave wisdom to Solomon, just as
> he had promised. And Hiram and Solomon made a
> formal alliance of peace.   (1 Kings 5:12)

His wisdom brought peace. Through this wisdom he made strategic political alliances to garner support for his efforts. This is the wisdom that Solomon employed to complete the work of the Temple and dedicate it to the Lord before all Israel. This is the wisdom that also allowed him to have an answer for everything.

> He composed some 3,000 proverbs and wrote
> 1,005 songs. He could speak with authority about
> all kinds of plants, from the great cedar of Lebanon
> to the tiny hyssop that grows from cracks in a wall.
> He could also speak about animals, birds, small
> creatures, and fish.   (1 Kings 4:32-33)

We have the Book of Proverbs which places much of this wisdom on display. This wisdom went beyond judging the affairs of man fairly, but also included an understanding of the world surrounding Solomon. This is the wisdom that "kings from every nation sent their ambassadors to listen to" (1 Kings 4:34) as Solomon's fame spread.

On one occasion, a wise and powerful queen sought him out to meet him in person by way of Sheba. She actually came with a bunch of questions to test his wisdom and "nothing was too hard for the king to explain to her" (1 Kings 10:3). His wisdom was so palpable it was able to be seen (v. 4) and took her breath away (v. 5).

> She exclaimed to the king, "Everything I heard in
> my country about your achievements and wisdom
> is true! I didn't believe what was said until I arrived
> here and saw it with my own eyes. In fact, I had not
> heard the half of it! Your wisdom and prosperity are
> far beyond what I was told."   (1 Kings 10:6-7)

She ended up dropping several tons of gold, jewels, and

spices on him because she was so moved. And such as it was for Solomon, he was rolling in cold, hard cash because all of the visitors who heard of his wisdom and fame would lavish him with gifts (see 1 Kings 10:14-25). Let's just put it out there: what Solomon asked for made him rich and famous.

You're saying, "Okay, we get it—wisdom is important. In order to be good stewards, we need wisdom."

So did Solomon.

You see, Solomon wanted to do a good job. And through his story, it appeared as if he had every intention of doing so. It's also hard to argue with the results: he built the Temple, a royal palace, several towns and national landmarks. And there was that time when even God showed up and gave him a high-five.

> The Lord said to him,
> "I have heard your prayer and your petition. I have set this Temple apart to be holy—this place you have built where my name will be honored forever. I will always watch over it, for it is dear to my heart.
> (1 Kings 9:3)

In chapter 8, Solomon prayed a prayer—almost as nice as his father David's—asking God to bless the Temple and the people who worshipped and prayed in it and to confirm the promise that "one of [their descendants] will always sit on the throne of Israel" (1 Kings 8:25). God's response to Solomon's reminder was a reminder of His own—that Solomon would need to walk it out to see the promise.

> And as for you, if you will walk before me, as David your father walked, with integrity of heart and uprightness, doing according to all that I have commanded you, and keeping my statutes and my rules ...   (1 Kings 9:4 ESV)

That's a big *if*.

Let's get real. Following his request to God, much of the story of Solomon shows the wisdom of the head at work. He had the brains and the knowledge and all the answers; head, head, head. As we progress in reading Solomon's story, we begin to see his initially *good* motives begin to deteriorate. What was the "all" that God commanded Solomon? What were the statutes and rules? Here's just one set:

> "The king must not build up a large stable of horses for himself or send his people to Egypt to buy horses, for the Lord has told you, 'You must never return to Egypt.' The king must not take many wives for himself, because they will turn his heart away from the Lord. And he must not accumulate large amounts of wealth in silver and gold for himself."   (Deuteronomy 17:16-17)

Following the tales of his wealth, 1 Kings 10 gives us some insight into the life and reign of Solomon. Immediately you'll see that his stable was full of horses (v. 26) and they were from Egypt (v. 28). Turn the page and we read how he also collected his women.

> He had 700 wives of royal birth and 300 concubines. And in fact, they did turn his heart away from the Lord.   (1 Kings 11:3)

This is just one small set of rules (and the first set for a king in Israel). We can see the Lord was interested in Solomon's goodness, not just his greatness. *Khokhmah* is given to do God's will. This is not *khokhmah*.

WHAT COULD BE BETTER?

If we were to track backward in Solomon's story, we would see that his father David was "sought out" by God as "a man after his own heart" (see 1 Samuel 13:14). And David was by no means a perfect man. The beauty we see in David is found in the God whose heart he was chasing after. Through his mistakes and tragedies, King David chose to remain close to God, even though in his darkest hour he felt God had turned His back on him (see Psalm 13). David figured, if he didn't have the Lord on his side, he was doomed anyway. There wasn't another option.

Which leads to Solomon's request—was it the best possible response to God's open-ended petition? If by studying the life of David and discerning what made him great, we discover that it was the very presence of God that made him the victorious leader he was, then what's the number one thing we could ask for? Better than an understanding heart. Better than doing a good job. Better than a knowledge of good and evil, right from wrong.

God was pleased by Solomon's request because it went beyond the superficial desires commonly found in the heart of man. In 1 Kings 3:11, He reveals resources we all wish for: time ("a long life"), money ("wealth"), and respect ("the death of your enemies"). I feel like this list can be found in the warning section in a book about genies. And you can't wish for more wishes. A heart that discerns right from wrong is certainly a greater resource than these, but Adam and Eve could tell you that knowledge of good and evil isn't the greatest. They enjoyed the completeness of the greatest resource known to man—fellowship with God.

God Himself is far greater than the gifts He can give us. Do you really believe that? The chance to experience a closeness to the Father like David had before Solomon and as Jesus had before us is the best thing we can ask for. And as I mentioned before, those of us who have chosen to rely on Jesus for our complete salvation already have this incredible opportunity. Yet many believers still go through life leaving the best gifts on the table because they lack the character to seize it. You were not made (or remade) for a subpar walk with Christ.

The *Big If* for Solomon meant that in order to see what he was praying for, he would need to surrender what he determined was right in his own head for what he found was right according to God's Word. That's the heart of Proverbs 3:5-6, saying, "Trust in the Lord with all your heart; do not depend on your own understanding. Seek his will in all you do, and he will show you which path to take." The same goes for us now:

if we are going to *use well* the opportunity to glorify God in our finances, we're going to have to get out of our own heads.

GETTING OUT OF YOUR OWN HEAD

There is something innately attractive about confidence. We all have an internal meter that reads others' words and tests the truth of their claims. To a degree, we can tell when someone believes what they're actually saying. That is why my classmates continued to come to me for advice. With an elementary observation of my environment, I could confidently say things that were generally confirmed through the patterns of the world. But were the proverbs I gave *that* profound or were they drawn to me because I was *that* confident?

What are you confident in? Much of the time, what we believe is based on what we are able to observe. Other times, we believe what feels appropriate. The danger arrives when these beliefs become our doctrine. It's natural for us to marry these belief systems and before we know it, they become unwavering principles that we choose to live by.

I'm not going to say I was ever wrong when it came to giving my classmates advice—I'll just say that there's quite a number of variables when it comes to healthy relationships and they can't easily be summed up based on all that's free to observe or that feels appropriate. So stuff happened. Things that no one could predict got in the way. Eventually, all the newly fabricated couples I set up, broke up. Teenage summers are tough, right?

In the midst of your own self-made theories, you've also got a lot of unseen variables. We create these belief systems for a reason—to protect ourselves from the pain of failure, to give us closure about the unknown, and to point us toward what's best. But if we are going to be unwavering in the way we navigate life, wouldn't it be better if we take into account the things that can't be seen?

In the seventh grade, I had dozens of unwritten rules that would govern how I saw the world. Little did I know, I became married to these doctrinal beliefs; I was loyal to a fault. As the years went by, my relationship toward these proverbs only grew deeper and I acquired even more spouses—hundreds in fact—and like Solomon, they eventually led me away from the security and the knowledge of the heart of God. What's worse, after high school, I made many of these "wise teachings" into words of encouragement for my peers with scriptural backing. And one day, I was forced to come to grips with the fact that my formulas could be missing God's valuable input. What do you do when you come upon new information that challenges your old self-made doctrine?

New rule: in the case of *My Opinion vs. Anything Jesus Said*, Jesus wins.

Check out the dilemma Paul was dealing with when he wrote the Corinthian church:

> So where does this leave the philosophers, the scholars, and the world's brilliant debaters? God has made the wisdom of this world look foolish. Since God in his wisdom saw to it that the world would never know him through human wisdom, he has used our foolish preaching to save those who believe. It is foolish to the Jews, who ask for signs from heaven. And it is foolish to the Greeks, who seek human wisdom. So when we preach that Christ was crucified, the Jews are offended and the Gentiles say it's all nonsense.(1 Corinthians 1:20-23)

Paul sarcastically called his preaching of the Good News "foolish" in comparison to the underlying belief systems of those he was called to share it with. The message was to go first to the Jews and then to the other nations; Paul found that although they thought differently, they both had to overcome a mental hurdle to receive the message with joy and splendor. The Jews didn't think it lofty enough; the story of Jesus was too human. The Gentiles thought it was too shallow; it didn't exercise enough intellectual finesse.

> But to those called by God to salvation, both Jews and Gentiles, Christ is the power of God and the wisdom of God.　　　　(1 Corinthians 1:24)

Paul reminds the people of the Church in Corinth that they were different. For them, Christ satisfied the loftiness of deity and the depth of the human thought. He then used them as an illustration:

> Remember, dear brothers and sisters, that few of you were wise in the world's eyes or powerful or wealthy when God called you. Instead, God chose things the world considers foolish in order to shame those who think they are wise. And he chose things that are powerless to shame those who are powerful.   (1 Corinthians 1:26-27)

Paul knows these folks well enough to keep it real with them. You guys are called to teach the whole world—great and small—the way of Jesus Christ. No one on earth is wise enough for that task. Especially not these people. (Watch your toes!) When God called you, you weren't much to write home about, either. And yet, that was the plan of God all along. Those who remain stuck in their own heads, married to their own wisdom, get in their own way of seeing Jesus for who He is. The world might call you rich or powerful or a scholar but counting on these things is what the Bible defines as foolish.

Based on the way the chapter ends, it seems Paul had Jeremiah 9 in mind as he wrote that explanation. If our goals include increasing every means to the Ultimate End (Jesus), at some point, the world will have reason to celebrate us because of riches, fame, or intelligence. You are destined to become a *have* one day. But if we count on any of that to define who we are more than the identity we receive from God, we make the same mistake that Solomon made.

> This is what the Lord says: "Don't let the wise boast in their wisdom, or the powerful boast in their power, or the rich boast in their riches. But those who wish to boast should boast in this alone: that they truly know me and understand that I am the Lord who demonstrates unfailing love and who brings justice and righteousness to the earth,

> and that I delight in these things. I, the Lord, have
> spoken!"   (Jeremiah 9:23-24)

There's something to be said about truly knowing your God. As was said about David, he was after God's heart. Intimacy with God the Father is far greater than head knowledge. You may entertain kings and queens from distant lands, impressing them with your life, insight, and understanding, but wise believers will see this as a "use well" opportunity to introduce them to a God who loves eternally and delights in making wrong things right (justice and righteousness).

Do people leave your life the same as how they entered it? If you find that many of the people in your life have good things to say about you but they're unaffected by your relationship with God, you may be leaving a Solomon-sized portion of wisdom on the table. We ought to desire the Gift-Giver more than the gifts themselves.

Even if you are currently walking in close fellowship with God, pray that prayer again tomorrow and benefit even more. And if you truly want wisdom to manifest through that relationship, it will take character to sustain you.

12

THE ONLY THING TO FEAR

For God has not given us a spirit of fear and timidity, but of power, love, and self-discipline. —2 Timothy 1:7

We just spent a great deal of time talking about Solomon, but I'm not letting you off the hook just yet—we still have to deal with that third servant. Have you ever felt like that one-talent servant? Have you ever felt like, by comparison to others, you weren't given enough, whether it's money, skills, ability, knowledge, good looks, discipline, healthy relationships, or attention span? Or how about just feeling way in over your head, according to your comfort level? That's such a tough place to live, and it's where we become gripped with fear and come to God only with excuses. Fear is crippling; fear is paralyzing. How do we make wise financial decisions with such pressure?

Allow me to illustrate like this. Say I take my keys and toss them over to you and say, "Here are the keys to my car. Take care of it as if it were your own." That wouldn't be an extreme request, right? We all do something like this at some point.

I've heard many commended like this: "I love my stepfather; he cared for me as if I were his own." "My neighbor takes care of our dogs as if they were her own."

What are we saying when we do this? We take note when someone demonstrates that they value what's valuable to us. My car is valuable to me. When I toss you the keys, I'm saying that I trust you; you know me, and I know you. I trust you as an equal to take care of my car the same way (or better than) I take care of my car. Once you catch my keys, you'll find that my car is a nearly old enough to get a license and drive on its own. And when you start it up, you'll notice it's driven a fair amount of miles and is on its second motor. Chances are, your car is in better shape. Perhaps that takes some of the pressure off. If so, give me my keys back because I need you to see value in what I value.

> *Stewardship isn't taking care of someone's property as if it were yours, but taking care of their property as if you were them.*

That leads to relationship. If I can't trust you to take care of my car, what am I to do? Some people don't take care of their own stuff, so what then? I don't care how good the relationship is—when we don't trust, we withhold. But that's not really stewardship, is it? I'm not giving you the keys expecting you to take care of my car the same way you would take care of your own.

Stewardship isn't taking care of someone's property as if it were yours, but taking care of their property as if you were them. I remember sitting at lunch in the break room when a fellow co-worker left her purse with me and instructed, "Guard this with your life," as if it were a higher calling. Please! Let's be real, I don't know you like that! And the truth is, even if I did know you like that, I'm not dying for your purse. And if we're totally honest, she wouldn't even die for her *own* purse. Can you tell I was offended?

You see, relationship is important. But when God gives to us, He's never giving to an equal with an ability to take the same kind of care He can; He's always giving to a lesser. So what are we supposed to do? Imagine you catch those keys but you see they belong to a brand new Tesla Model S with all the options. Imagine it's no longer me tossing you the keys but instead it's descended to you from heaven.

Perhaps you hear that and think to yourself, "Sweet!" and then begin planning your high-speed Holy Spirit adventure. This probably isn't your chapter—but maybe it should be.

The rest of us felt the stakes change in that moment. This is right about the point where most of us start to feel like that one talent servant.

Why? Because now you have to deal with the idea: what if you crashed God's Tesla?

If it was God's *bicycle*, I wouldn't want to scuff it up. If God tosses me the keys to a Tesla and says, "Here you go. You know what to do," I'm terrified. But God knows he's giving to a lesser and He doesn't let go of the keys because of what exists in us, but because of the wisdom that exists in Him.

I realize this is totally something a bad driver would say, but I'm not a bad driver. I'm confident in my own skills; it's everyone else I'm worried about. I can't control the drunk drivers and red-light runners out there. Or how about all the folks texting and driving, veering from lane to lane? And then there's the ever-increasing number of potholes the city still hasn't attempted to fix. That's what freaks me out. I'm not getting on the road in God's Tesla with all those hazards I just can't control.

Is it starting to sound like I'm making excuses? Let's call it what it is: *fear*. What do we do when we're fearful? We end up doing one of two things: either we avoid taking any risk, or we become consumed with worry and miss the experience. Either way, we never experience the full potential of the provision when we espouse fear. So we keep God's Tesla parked in the garage and never take it outside. Or we take it out, but only in the neighborhood and on the side streets—we never get it up to speed, and we wouldn't dare get on the freeway.

When God returns, He might ask, "How was it?" Can you imagine the disappointment when we say that we never took it for a spin? We chose to *do nothing* rather than to *use well*. All because we feared failure more than we feared the Lord.

> Then the servant with the one bag of silver came and said, "Master, I knew you were a harsh man, harvesting crops you didn't plant and gathering crops you didn't cultivate. I was afraid I would lose your money, so I hid it in the earth. Look, here is your money back."   (Matthew 25:24-25)

The third servant started his presentation to his master with "I knew you." What did he know about his master? For one, he was not an easy man to please. To say he harvested and gathered crops he didn't plant makes me think of two possibilities: either he benefits from the labor of others or he is *hashtag blessed*, scattering seed in one place and getting an unexpected harvest somewhere else. Either way, the standards are high.

"I knew you" is a great start in explaining the reasoning behind how we manage what we are given. What do you know about your God who has entrusted to you all that you have—material and immaterial? What if what you think you know about God is insufficient, or even worse, inimical to Him altogether? Does that influence the way you manage those allotments? Interestingly enough, what the third servant "knew" about the master wasn't enough to motivate him to do what the master would do. True fear of the Lord should prompt the opposite effect in us.

FEAR IN LOVE?

The fear of the Lord is expressed over 120 times in the Bible in one form or another and implied even more. With such a strong emphasis on the subject, we get that it's important, but we don't really know why or what that means for us. The English language can be tricky at times. Most people can quote, "Fear of the Lord is the beginning of wisdom" and many have heard the phrase "a healthy fear of God." But even more people know that "God so loved the world" and that "God is love" and that "there is no fear in love." We cling to scriptures where we're instructed to "fear not" and psalms that give us courage to overcome any fear. "Of whom shall I be afraid?"

The Lord.

That's it. Of all the scriptures that suggest we should not fear, none of them contradict the overarching theme of fearing God. But because we don't read the Bible as a whole story, we often miss these major lessons wedged in between passages. This lack then requires us to use our own understanding of fear to define what the Word intends us to develop as part of the process of being discipled.

The dictionary has several definitions for fear and so do we. We like to believe that there's a type of fear reserved for things that are dangerous and scary and another for good things like parents and God. If someone or something has the ability to inflict pain on you, aww man, that's scary. If you hold a deep respect for the wisdom of your elders, aww, that's sweet.

No matter how you spell it, there is really only one kind of fear: Ahh! Sure, there are varying degrees and several different ways you may respond but internally, your soul is screaming, "Oh crap! Hey self, this could kill us." Some mighty and powerful things strike awe in us and have no intention of killing us. We usually don't recognize our approach to these things as fear because we set boundaries to protect ourselves.

Take planes, trains, or automobiles, for instance. The highway is flooded with millions of two-ton, fire-breathing death traps hurtling about in every direction. On most roads, the only separation between you and another steel juggernaut moving in the opposite direction is a painted suggestion. We keep our wild, mechanical carriages in line as if those impalpable markings were drill sergeants. And because we prefer our lives, we honor them as we seek to traverse one of their man-eating pits by foot. We call it a crosswalk. But we're really just cloaking our fear with a mask of safety and caution.

Is it any different for God? Let's look at some cases, starting with the time Moses first came to Sinai.

> There the angel of the Lord appeared to him in a blazing fire from the middle of a bush. Moses stared in amazement. Though the bush was engulfed in flames, it didn't burn up. "This is amazing," Moses said to himself. "Why isn't that bush burning up? I must go see it."
>
> When the Lord saw Moses coming to take a closer look, God called to him from the middle of the bush, "Moses! Moses!"
>
> "Here I am!" Moses replied.
>
> "Do not come any closer," the Lord warned. "Take off your sandals, for you are standing on holy ground. I am the God of your father —the God of Abraham, the God of Isaac, and the God of Jacob." When Moses heard this, he covered his face because he was afraid to look at God.(Exodus 3:3-6)

In another instance, as Moses rescued his people Israel from Egypt and led them out by way of the Red Sea, God showed up, held back the sea to carve out a dry path to the other side, and disrupted the Egyptian army in hot pursuit. As soon as Israel made it across, the sea was released and Egypt's finest were drowned in the chaotic water.

> When the people of Israel saw the mighty power that the Lord had unleashed against the Egyptians, they were filled with awe before him. They put their faith in the Lord and in his servant Moses.
>
> (Exodus 14:31)

"They were filled with awe," but the original text says "they feared the Lord." (Apparently, "they peed their pants" would have been too much of a stretch as a paraphrase for the NLT.) As if that wasn't scary enough, years later Moses took the people back to where it all began.

> Moses led them out from the camp to meet with God, and they stood at the foot of the mountain. All of Mount Sinai was covered with smoke because the Lord had descended on it in the form of fire. The smoke billowed into the sky like smoke from a brick kiln, and the whole mountain shook violently. As the blast of the ram's horn grew louder and louder, Moses spoke, and God thundered his reply.
> (Exodus 19:17-19)
> When the people heard the thunder and the loud blast of the ram's horn, and when they saw the flashes of lightning and the smoke billowing from the mountain, they stood at a distance, trembling with fear. And they said to Moses, "You speak to us, and we will listen. But don't let God speak directly to us, or we will die!"
> "Don't be afraid," Moses answered them, "for God has come in this way to test you, and so that your fear of him will keep you from sinning!"
> (Exodus 20:18-20)

Between those two above passages, God is audibly dictating the Ten Commandments directly to the people through the fire, smoke, earthquake, storm, thunder, and lightning. The people are right in thinking to themselves, *This could kill us.* Yet Moses says to them what we also find in many other passages when God shows up or sends an angel to meet a mortal in person: "Don't be afraid."

Are you crazy? A scary encounter with the supernatural and I'm not supposed to be afraid? Why would God say that? Why would the angels say that? Why would Jesus say that? Why does Moses say that? What does he know that we don't?

Moses knew of a fire that burned, but didn't consume. He knew of something powerful enough to kill us, yet that didn't want us to die. It's possible to fear God and not be afraid. See how A. W. Tozer put it in his aptly named Christian classic *The Knowledge of the Holy*:

> The greatness of God rouses fear within us, but His goodness encourages us not to be afraid of Him. To fear and not be afraid - that is the paradox of faith.[12]

God has a will, and your destruction is not a part of it. As kids, we all trusted in our parents' instincts to keep us alive more than we did their power to ... not keep us alive. We believe that God is good and that He desires a close relationship with us and therefore is on our side. This causes us to lean on His love in spite of His severity.

I am not saying God is any less loving because He can be scary, nor am I saying that God's severity doesn't matter. As the Maker of all things great, He is the greatest. Anything that great is scary. God is scary great. Yet as the Maker of all things good, He's the *goodest*. He is worthy of both praise and fear—of awe, aww, and ahh!

THE FOUNDATION OF WISDOM

I use all that to preface this section on obtaining a foundational fear of the Lord because most of the biblical authors who wrote about a fear of God probably thought it more like the previous section than the bubbly version of love commonly explained to us.

Fear of the Lord is more like bubble guts than butterflies.

When taught in church, if it's brought up at all, I often hear the fear of the Lord spoken of as reverence or respect. I don't disagree with that rendering, but this way easily allows us to file the phrase as a bullet point under the main item: *Love*. Yet as we think about what we're going to do with God's Tesla and what that third servant is going to do with his master's portion, I believe it's helpful to recall that God can be scary. If we're going to do what He calls *good* with the things He entrusts to us, we need *Severity* to have its own place in our inventories of what we know about our God. We like to say that love is more than a feeling. Well, fear is more than a reaction—it's a choice just like walking, listening, and obeying.

We have the capacity to look at a master who reaps where he didn't sow and gathers a harvest where he hasn't scattered seed and add our own judgment, calling him "harsh." In the parable, the master was not offended by this, rather he expressed that the "harsh" label should have spurred the servant into positive action.

> Fear of the Lord is the foundation of wisdom.
> Knowledge of the Holy One results in good
> judgment.   (Proverbs 9:10)

One of the things I love about the proverbs, and most Hebrew poetry in general, is that it's hard to miss the point. One familiar way for Hebrew poets to "rhyme" is not through repetition of sounds but repetition of ideas. So many proverbs and psalms feature lines that come in pairs and basically say the same thing twice in two different ways. This creates a poetic rhythm while sealing the pith of its argument. For nerds like me, it allows for great word-and-phrase association, too. Like in the passage above, "fear of the Lord" is compared with "knowledge of the Holy One" and "wisdom" is compared with "good judgment." In the last chapter, we talked about how wisdom relates to good judgment, and in this chapter we've focused on fear of God and how it relates to having knowledge of the Holy One. See the pattern?

In reading through the Old Testament, it is evident that God, the writers, and the readers believed a fear of the Lord could be taught. So here is my attempt to pass the teaching along in a few points outlined in scripture.

Read God's Word daily (Deuteronomy 17:19). A king was instructed to make a copy of the law (as much of a Bible as they had at the time) and "read it daily as long as he lives. That way he will learn to fear the Lord his God." Whether it was through the uprightness of piety or the shame of ineptitude, the habit of continual reading was a prescription for healthy fear.

**Unleash your memory and testimony (Deuteronomy 4:9-

10). Etched into Jewish tradition is passing on the incredible story of God choosing Israel. How God met you where you were and initiated a relationship with you is a story you should rehearse and pass on. Moses urged the people, "Be careful to never forget what you yourself have seen ... Never forget the day when you stood before the Lord your God at Mount Sinai." God said that as they regularly recalled their encounter, "they will learn to fear me as long as they live, and they will teach their children to fear me also." It is far more likely that we will forget what God did in the past than not encounter Him in the future. Fear for the future is evidence that what God did in the past has lost its power in us.

Dedicate your first and best to God (Deuteronomy 14:23 ESV). Though this tithe is set aside for God, notice who consumes it. God explains, "before the Lord your God ... you shall eat the tithe" which consisted of "your grain, of your wine, and of your oil, and the firstborn of your herd and flock," concluding "that you may learn to fear the Lord your God always." Trusting the Lord for your increase and enjoying a portion in His honor will ensure that you'll need to trust Him all the more.

Be accountable to others (Deuteronomy 31:12-13). Not only does a regular reading of Scripture teach us to fear the Lord, but it helps when those around you share the same standards. Every seventh year, Israel was to assemble all their people and listen to the audio Bible "so that [their] children who have not known these instructions will hear them and will learn to fear the Lord your God." Imagine a land where no one could use the excuse "I didn't know" and everyone was clear on how *you* should act. That's what it's like when you run with a circle of people who share your faith and are familiar with your values. It doesn't hurt to start a Bible reading plan with this circle, either.

Pray expecting an answer (1 Kings 8:43). Solomon knew "all the people of the earth will come to know and fear [the Lord]" when they saw God hear from heaven and respond to their prayers.

Acquaint yourself with forgiveness (Psalm 130:3-4). If we got into the habit of forgiving others, we'd have to wrestle more often with the duality of mercy and justice. We think we want justice, but not when it comes to our own wrongs. As the psalmist put it, a record of our sins would mean certain ruin, but God offers "forgiveness, that we might learn to fear [Him]." Forgiveness doesn't declare you not guilty, it just lets the guilty off the hook. Our flesh wants to pay for doing wrong, but God prefers we learn His ways.

Learn from the experts (Psalm 34:11). If you're willing to listen and humble yourself as a child, mentors and elders have treasure troves of wisdom hidden by God.

Seek wisdom (Proverbs 2:2-5). There are a lot of nuggets of wisdom out there. If you "search for them as you would for silver … then you will understand what it means to fear the Lord."

As we increase in our knowledge of the Holy One, so will our fear of the Lord be made pure. As we increase in our fear of the Lord, so will wisdom—our potential to judge what is right and do it—rise to the surface. That is because what we know about God *is* the very fear we have of Him. The fear we have of God *is* the very wisdom we seek. Job said it like this:

> "God alone understands the way to wisdom; he knows where it can be found, for he looks throughout the whole earth and sees everything under the heavens. He decided how hard the winds should blow and how much rain should fall. He made the laws for the rain and laid out a path for the lightning. Then he saw wisdom and evaluated it. He set it in place and examined it thoroughly. And this is what he says to all humanity: 'The fear of the Lord is true wisdom; to forsake evil is real understanding.'" (Job 28:23-28)

In the Book of Job, Job and his friends share long speeches of their knowledge of God, yet because they are unaware of what happened in the first two chapters, they miss how to apply it. While their belief in God and His justice are mostly true, the conclusions they draw are all wrong. Speaking so matter-of-factly about things they couldn't know without going to Him ultimately showed the lack of fear they had of the Lord.

Think about what God has revealed to you about Himself. Are those things encouraging you to do right by Him or keeping His desires for you parked? Sometimes just the way you see God makes all the difference. Is the God you know a loving Father to you? Perhaps you only see Him as a "harsh" disciplinarian. That may mean you're missing the fact that "the Lord corrects those he loves, just as a father corrects a child in whom he delights" (see Proverbs 3:12). The third servant knew about his master's "never lose" attitude but drew a wrong conclusion as to what that meant for him.

The master couldn't accept the excuses of the servant, knowing what the servant knew about him. He states, if the servant really knew him, he would have known that the opportunity came with great expectations. Likewise, our Master isn't open to our excuses knowing what we know about Him. He hasn't misappropriated our portions because He knows our limitations, but He also knows our potential so He's expecting a return.

Here's the truth about the blessing God has given you: it was never meant for you to keep it to yourself. You don't need a million-dollar jackpot or miracle car keys to consider what kind of manager He wants you to be. If everything you have now belongs to God (which it does) and one day will all return to Him (which it will), how would He want you to be putting those things to good use?

Don't leave His car sitting in the garage. Fear the Lord.

Similar to the idea of house sitting: you get the benefit of living in a space where nothing belongs to you because that space is supposed to bring more glory to the owner by you being present than when it's left vacant. So let's not be foolish about this; let's understand the Owner better. A genuine relationship with God is the key to developing a healthy fear of the Lord. Fear of the Lord is something that should motivate us to trust our God-given abilities to add value to our portion and inspire us to obedience to His Word.

When we fear the Lord, we are driven by His perspective and our desire is to *use well*. And we don't know what *well* is until we know what God knows *well* to be. When we fear lesser things—such as lack, poverty, failure, reputation, or people—it drives us to foolishness, and we *do nothing*.

> "Now throw this useless servant into outer darkness, where there will be weeping and gnashing of teeth." (Matthew 25:30)

Wait. What?

13

WE'RE NOT TALKING ABOUT MONEY, ARE WE?

Why can't you understand that I'm not talking about bread? —Matthew 16:11

It's probably obvious at this point that we're not talking about money at all. Parables were never meant to tell the obvious story, anyway. Remember, Jesus would first share the story that everyone could understand. Then He would draw His disciples' attention to the meaning.

Because we are so far removed from the culture of the original audience of the parables, we often spend quite a bit of time in our studies and at the pulpit explaining the concepts within the content of the parables and what they mean. This is necessary if we're going to understand what was so notable or controversial about a story Jesus told. Of course, if we lived in that time, none of those things would need explaining. So we must fill in the concepts but we also lack the context and the subtext surrounding the parables.

One or more of these gaps often goes unaddressed when we dive into Jesus's parables. It almost happened in this book—I spent a considerable amount of time explaining the concepts within the parable and we only briefly touched on the context. Context is key if we're to know whether we're rightly understanding God's Word. And it's the underlying messages that the disciples would beg Jesus to explain in greater detail. They help us to know whether we're rightly applying God's Word.

If you want the subtext (meaning *woven underneath*) you've got two options: to dig for a deeper understanding of yourself or for a deeper understanding of the God you serve. We started this process at the beginning of this book and will touch on it as we close. You will notice subtext every time you encounter the Scriptures in light of the words we defined. If you want to discover the context (meaning *woven together*), you need a deeper understanding of the passage, the writer, and the intended audience. One way to do this is to study the culture and literature of the time period. We can't do that here, but it would prove to be very enlightening if you were so inclined. We can, however, find some of that context within the text by reading what comes before and after the passage.

READ ALL ABOUT IT

Let's try that with The Parable of the Three Servants. This passage is no different when it comes to a deep-seated message. Although Jesus is using finances to illustrate stewardship, that is only the superficial explanation of the parable; He's not really teaching about finances at all. Let's go further—He's not really teaching about stewardship, either.

This can't be a complete representation of stewardship opportunities. With the number of people in debt today, why else do we not see what happens when a servant loses his master's money? And for those of us who are financially average: if this *were* a parable about money, wouldn't you like to see a fourth servant who got three or four bags of silver, put them to use, lost a couple in some bad investments, but still had something to bring to the table? There's got to be more to this parable than meets the eye.

Okay, that last paragraph was filtered by my personal context. In order to understand the true context, we're looking for the who, what, when, where, and why. Earlier, we read how Jesus would share these types of stories in front of the crowds and then explain them when He got alone with His disciples. Let's answer a few questions about this passage.

Who was the crowd? There's no indication in Chapter 25; just a lot of red text. If you read backward from the parable, you'll see even more red text. What we find is that Jesus was teaching at the Temple and He was getting challenged by both the Pharisees and Sadducees and judged by the religious leaders (see Chapters 21 and 22). In Matthew 23:1, we read, "Then Jesus said to the crowds and to his disciples ..." After that scathing indictment (check it out later—great bathroom reading), Jesus left the Temple with His trusted few (see Matthew 24:1).

> Later, Jesus sat on the Mount of Olives. His disciples came to him privately and said, "Tell us, when will all this happen? What sign will signal your return and the end of the world?   (Matthew 24:3)

The disciples were the *who*, verse 3 says the Mount of Olives was the *where*, and then they asked Him the *when* and *what*. What follows is the response Jesus gave to His disciples. And perhaps we see yet another reason why Jesus preferred to use parables. In Matthew 24 starting in verse 4, He begins to answer their question quite plainly. I can imagine Him seeing their eyes glaze over right about the part where angels come "with a loud trumpet call, and they will gather his elect from the four winds, from one end of heaven to the other" (v. 31 ESV).

From that point on, Jesus shifts to parables. Even though He was speaking to His disciples, Jesus determined it was the best way to continue explaining His point. If you read further, it makes a lot of sense, too. Jesus is about to explain the replacement of the heaven and earth we know with a New Heaven and New Earth yet unseen. And that's consistent with much of biblical content up to this time; anytime it speaks of things that are out of this world (literally), Scripture uses allusions of what we know on earth to reflect what we might know beyond this world.

So yes, instead of plainly explaining the parables with teaching, Jesus uses the parables in Chapter 25 as symbols to explain what He taught earlier in Chapters 21 through 23. He also needed to reiterate what He explained in Chapter 24, which was all about the Kingdom of God at the end of the age.

IF YOU STAY READY

What will it be like, when will it happen, and how will we know? Those are the questions that bubbled up as Jesus warned all who would hear Him. I'll save the full explanation of the concepts within the End Time parables for another book; hopefully one written by someone much smarter than me. But there are a few things we do know for sure.

Firstly, the world as we see it today is eventually going to come to an end. It's not clear exactly how, but there will be a day in the foreseeable future where what exists now will either exist differently or cease to exist completely in a snap. Jesus explains that "it will be like it was in Noah's day" (Matthew 24:37), meaning it will look like an average day immediately before everything changes.

Secondly, no one knows when it's going to all go down; just know it's going down. It's at this point and all that follows where Jesus keeps speaking about going away for an unspecified length of time and returning unannounced. He instructs that "we must be ready all the time, for the Son of Man will come when least expected" (Matthew 24:44).

As Suga Free puts it (another '90s hip-hop reference): "If you stay ready, you ain't got to get ready."

From this point on, Jesus tells a series of stories that share similar themes. There's a master, a bridegroom, and a man. In three different scenarios, there are people who are given responsibilities; some are deemed wise, while others are declared foolish. One thing that all three stories share alike: there's an un-specified period of time the people must wait, followed by further delay. Jesus is posing the question, *Who will stay ready?*

The very next verse says this:

> A faithful, sensible servant is one to whom the master can give the responsibility of managing his other household servants and feeding them.
> (Matthew 24:45)

This is the start of an easily overlooked parable, probably because the text it's surrounded by is more popular and quotable. But notice the key that Jesus gives; it may even unlock some of the wording in the Parable of the Three Servants. In that parable, two of the servants are called "good and faithful" while this one here is called "faithful and sensible." The word *sensible* speaks to wisdom; they actually share the same Greek root word. It just makes logical sense to serve your master with respect to the unknown, yet very near, time of his return.

Growing up, there were always a few weeks right after school let out for the summer but before any summer programs started, when my mom would leave my older brother and me at the house while she went to work. Even better, with so much time on our hands, she would give each of us a chore to complete before she got home.

Like clockwork, the sound of the garage door opening would be the abrupt reminder that I was done for. (Eight hours seems like so much more time when you're in class.) I had one job. Besides taking more than ten seconds to vacuum the entire house, I was to make sure that when my mom got home, it didn't look like we had been playing video games all day long—that's it. I wish I could say I was more sensible, but I even tried this once or twice: "You see, I vacuumed the house as soon as I got up but it's been so long since, that it just doesn't *look* vacuumed in here anymore."

That didn't fly *then* and it surely won't when Jesus comes back. You know how this is going to end. If you stay ready, you won't have to get ready. In Luke's account of the same parable, he provides an alternate ending to the story with additional insight.

> And a servant who knows what the master wants, but isn't prepared and doesn't carry out those instructions, will be severely punished. But someone who does not know, and then does something wrong, will be punished only lightly. When someone has been given much, much will be required in return; and when someone has been entrusted with much, even more will be required.   (Luke 12:47-48)

Full disclosure, the context here suggests Jesus is talking about God's long history with Israel, who should know God well enough to do what He would want done. Remember the fear of the Lord? Same principle applies here, although you could argue that we have record of an even greater revelation since all of this took place prior to Christ's resurrection. We now have the testimony of the apostles in our New Testament. It is imperative that we observe our Lord well enough to know what He wants.

Notice how we see more of the "to those who ..." type language in this passage, only this time it speaks to responsibility and punishment. Here He claims some are "given much" while others are "entrusted with much," and the item in question is knowledge of what the Master wants. Not to add any weight to your chains, but if you're reading this book, you most likely don't need convincing you fall into the latter category.

Jesus continues in Matthew 25 with a parable about ten bridesmaids. Half of them were labeled foolish since they didn't plan for a possible delay. (It's sad; go read it.) And then, we're brought to the Parable of the Three Servants in verses 14 through 30.

As you can see, the Parable of the Three Servants is about the last days—from the time the Master leaves on His trip until the day He returns—and we're living in that time. We don't know how far we are into the "delay" but this does raise some other questions. What does that mean for us? What has Jesus entrusted us with? And what does He expect us "good and faithful" servants to do while He's away?

It seems Jesus is handing out investment advice if we're willing to follow it.

Are there any bad investments within the Kingdom of God? It doesn't look like it. According to Jesus, the Kingdom is the only good investment we can make! Considering the last three parables, knowing what the Master wants and doing it is a guaranteed recipe for success. Anything less is not the Kingdom.

If I told you there was a commodity that came at a fairly high cost today, but soon—I can't tell you exactly when, but very soon—it will quickly plummet and be worth absolutely nothing, would you buy in? Would you go all in? That's a senseless deal, right?

ALL IN

We know full well that the treasures of this world have nothing eternal to offer. Riches, fame, beauty, houses, cars, clothes, jobs, diet, sexual expression, and entertainment are just the beginning of a list of categories the world opens up to us. We know that these things are empty and fleeting but this is a concept we'd prefer to know in theory rather than learn firsthand.

> Then Jesus turned to his disciples and said, "God blesses you who are poor, for the Kingdom of God is yours.
> "What sorrow awaits you who are rich, for you have your only happiness now."   (Luke 6:20,24)

Oh, how I wish Jesus wasn't saying what it sounds like He's saying! Jesus begins with "blessed are you" (you know you grew up in church if you just read that *bless-id*). Moving on, look at the items in the list that follow. You are blessed if you are "hungry now," "weep now," and "when people hate you." This is a comparative list, meaning all of its items are similar. If Jesus was contrasting things that were different, context would tell us and we would see Him highlight two opposite things. Technically,

He's doing this on a broader scale by juxtaposing this list with the sorrows in verses 24-26. So it's reasonable to believe Jesus considered all of the listed blessings as similar in some way. But how?

For one, they're all blessings—privileges that not everyone gets to experience. Secondly, all of these conditions are temporary; notice the emphasis on the words "now" and "when." As Jesus is naming off a list of transient things, wealth is the only one He assumed didn't need a temporal modifier. Wealth, just like hunger and weeping, comes and goes. The rich and the poor, the revered and the reviled all experience a temporary status.

With all this in mind, many of us still have chosen to go all in with our investments of the world. I've had to consider where I first bought in, and I recall that I was taught the values of this world well before learning of the Kingdom of God. As an American, I was sold the American Dream, which promised *I could be anything I wanted to be if only I put my mind to it and worked hard enough*. That promise was then kindled with a mix of selfish ambition and keeping up with the Joneses. Perhaps your story is different, but I bet it's eerily similar. It's not wrong to dream, asking *Why Not?*, but apart from the will and the promises of God, what assurance do we have?

> "What sorrow awaits my rebellious children," says the Lord . "You make plans that are contrary to mine. You make alliances not directed by my Spirit, thus piling up your sins.
>
> For without consulting me, you have gone down to Egypt for help. You have put your trust in Pharaoh's protection. You have tried to hide in his shade.   (Isaiah 30:1-2)

This jumped out at me, to see that we weren't the only ones who used the world's system as a security blanket. Key phrase: "without consulting me." How many times have we asked God to bless our rebellion? We reason, because security is deemed a *good* thing (especially financial security), whatever is sure to offer security is worthy of our engagement. Why consult God about something that seems *good*? Ask Eve. A few verses later God describes through Isaiah what the scene looks like from His perspective, as God's people make an ancient bank transfer—going all in.

> ...The caravan moves slowly across the terrible desert to Egypt— donkeys weighed down with riches and camels loaded with treasure— all to pay for Egypt's protection. They travel through the wilderness, a place of lionesses and lions, a place where vipers and poisonous snakes live. All this, and Egypt will give you nothing in return.   (Isaiah 30:6)

This investment is headed "to Egypt, whose help is utterly useless. Therefore I call her Rahab the Do-Nothing" (v. 7 NIV). (Tell us how you really feel, God.) This was not a *use well* investment. At the top of the next chapter of Isaiah, the Lord offers a warning: "What sorrow awaits those who look to Egypt for help trusting their horses, chariots, and charioteers and depending on the strength of human armies instead of looking to the Lord" (Isaiah 31:1). Once again, this shows the importance of fearing the Lord. It's not a strength issue; it's a trust issue.

The children of God had every reason to search for their source of strength. Assyria had already come and flexed its muscles. Babylon was on the way to replace them. Egypt seemed like Israel's last hope of salvation. But Isaiah prophesied that like Assyria, Babylon would indeed fall. Was there no hope? Even more, Egypt was guaranteed to plummet just the same. Was this a good investment?

Ezekiel chapters 29-32 record several prophecies that mark Egypt for ruin. As Egypt was a symbol of the world's system of wealth and power, Babylon also shares this motif throughout the books of the prophets. God's people were carried off into into exile and spread among Babylonian cities. Generations later, they were all but assimilated into Babylonian culture. Their instructions from Jeremiah 29 were as follows:

> Build homes, and plan to stay. Plant gardens, and eat the food they produce. Marry and have children.

> Then find spouses for them so that you may have
> many grandchildren. Multiply! Do not dwindle
> away! And work for the peace and prosperity of the
> city where I sent you into exile. Pray to the Lord
> for it, for its welfare will determine your welfare.
>   (Jeremiah 29:5-7)

For the exiles, stewardship meant seeking the welfare of the great city without going "all in." They were to remain loyal in their worship and their trust. Jeremiah later prophesies in chapters 50 and 51 that Babylon will soon violently come crumbling down.

So what does all this have to do with today? From Genesis 11, Babylon has typified the place where humans have slapped God in the face. Anytime we desire to "preserve ourselves" and "make a name for ourselves," we invest In Babylon (see Genesis 11:4). The city was overtaken shortly after Jeremiah's prophecy but Babylon lives on in us.

THE OTHER MASTER

In a New Testament nod to the prophets, Revelation 18 offers a spoiler alert: Babylon is yet to fall. Read verses 9-19 to see the world's reaction; from all of the world leaders and customers and merchants and employees and beneficiaries of the fallen system—all weeping and wailing about their losses. If we're tied to the system, we will go down, too. Jesus's messages to His followers agree with this, giving light to His investment advice.

> "Don't store up treasures here on earth, where
> moths eat them and rust destroys them, and where
> thieves break in and steal. Store your treasures in
> heaven, where moths and rust cannot destroy, and
> thieves do not break in and steal."(Matthew 6:19-20)

Jesus paints the world and the Kingdom as two rival banks. He asserts that our hearts will be directed toward the account where we have the highest balance available.

> "Wherever your treasure is, there the desires of
> your heart will also be."   (Matthew 6:21)

Soon the things we desire begin to make our decisions for us. This is His conclusion:

> "No one can serve two masters. For you will hate
> one and love the other; you will be devoted to one
> and despise the other. You cannot serve God and be
> enslaved to money."   (Matthew 6:24)

In Luke 12, Jesus recounts the story of a man who has more than he needs. He explains the moral of the parable up front; that we should "guard against all covetousness, for one's life does not consist in the abundance of his possessions" (Luke 12:15 ESV).

> Then he told them a story: "A rich man had a
> fertile farm that produced fine crops. He said to
> himself, 'What should I do? I don't have room for
> all my crops.' Then he said, 'I know! I'll tear down
> my barns and build bigger ones. Then I'll have room
> enough to store all my wheat and other goods. And
> I'll sit back and say to myself, "My friend, you have
> enough stored away for years to come. Now take it
> easy! Eat, drink, and be merry!"'   (Luke 12:16-19)

We might find it tough to relate to this man for a few reasons. We don't live in an agrarian culture, we don't know what enough is, and as far as I'm concerned, my middle-class bank account can hold any amount I give it. Notice this other important tidbit: the man was called "rich" at the beginning of the story. Remember Chapter 1? You are rich folk—Jesus is talking about you. One thing that's easy to relate to is the rich man's hope for retirement. Why not store up enough for years to come? Isn't that what retirement is all about? There aren't many verses in the Bible that cover the issue of ceasing from our vocation at a certain age: as you get older, you either teach the next generation or you get taken care of by the next generation. And you never cease serving the Lord. The Bible is, however, loaded with verses on preparation. So the question becomes: what should we be preparing for?

> "But God said to him, 'You fool! You will die this very night. Then who will get everything you worked for?'"   (Luke 12:20)

The man's priorities were shown to be out of whack. He went all in on building *for himself*. He awakened Babylon. He trusted in the security of Egypt. He invested in Rahab the Do-Nothing. It all came to ruin. This should come as no surprise. We know that "everyone under the sun suffers the same fate" of mortality (see Ecclesiastes 9:2-3). If we do not live to hear the loud trumpet of Matthew 24, we'll see the events described in Ecclesiastes 9. Jesus concludes, "Yes, a person is a fool to store up earthly wealth but not have a rich relationship with God" (Luke 12:21).

The treasures of this world are temporary and will pass away but God is the Eternal One. Sure, we must be thinking ahead; we must be planning for our futures. After all, it is God who gives us vision to see that we may be wise to do His will. But if we lose sight of eternity in our planning, our plans are for naught. So when it comes to setting priorities for where we invest our time, money, and energy, everything that is guaranteed to give us nothing in return needs to be on the chopping block.

What is the appropriate response to a sure-fire flop? Not too long before writing this book, my laptop powered itself off and was slow to restart. Giving the slightest sign that it was going to kick the bucket, my instinct was to buy a new hard drive and copy all of my files over. When her refrigerator lost power, my grandma commissioned me to play Tetris, moving as much food from the kitchen to the "backup fridge" in the garage as possible. (What is it with grandmothers and multiple fridges?) Everything that could not fit, we had to give to the neighbors. Everything else was lost. At the news of the stock market crash of 2008, many responded in like fashion. *Take it out! It's all going down!* Time is of the essence; the sooner you get out, the less you stand to lose.

LIVING WITH PORPOISE

The writing is on the wall. We have our warning that the treasure this world offers is an obvious bait and switch. But do woke fish have any options in a society built on water? Suppose a shark came up to a dolphin and offered him some gills to breathe underwater. Should he take them? He was made to live within the system and he can navigate it well, but he wasn't made to go all in. His life is tuned in such a way that he must repeatedly and rhythmically come up for air. We would advise our woke fish, "Don't trust that shark!"

So what does "taking it out" look like in our scenario? I suppose it looks a lot like the exiles of Jeremiah 29 who lived for the benefit of a world they knew would eventually collapse. We are like the dolphin; contributing to an ecosystem—the only home it knows—but living by a different breath. When Jesus spoke of the Kingdom, He expressed that the alternative to buying into the earthly system is "storing up treasure in heaven." This is how we the rich can ditch the illegitimate gills we've been relying on. Later in Luke 12, Jesus spells it out plainly to His disciples.

> "Sell your possessions and give to those in need. This will store up treasure for you in heaven! And the purses of heaven never get old or develop holes. Your treasure will be safe; no thief can steal it and no moth can destroy it." (Luke 12:33)

Jesus said this same thing to the rich man who showed a sincere desire to partake in eternal life, running up to Jesus and throwing himself at His feet.

> Looking at the man, Jesus felt genuine love for him. "There is still one thing you haven't done," he told him. "Go and sell all your possessions and give

> the money to the poor, and you will have treasure in
> heaven. Then come, follow me."   (Mark 10:21)

I find myself reading passages like these and looking for alternate translations to achieve some sort of theological "balance." I know I'm not alone. We justify this by claiming that balance helps us avoid the extremes when in actuality, we're trying to avoid the Bible. There aren't enough verses in the book that could make "problem passages" not say what we don't want them to. That's a much called-for triple negative. Sometimes, the Bible is extreme. But remember that Jesus shares this with us out of "genuine love" for us. Help me out, Paul!

> Teach those who are rich in this world not to
> be proud and not to trust in their money, which
> is so unreliable. Their trust should be in God, who
> richly gives us all we need for our enjoyment. Tell
> them to use their money to do good. They should
> be rich in good works and generous to those in
> need, always being ready to share with others. By
> doing this they will be storing up their treasure as
> a good foundation for the future so that they may
> experience true life.   (1 Timothy 6:17-19)

Before you sell everything you own, listen to Paul's eloquent wordplay here to find "balance." If you've already sold everything, well, maybe it was meant to be. God will honor your heart. Selling it all is *not* a Kingdom requirement but trust (or faith) *is*. One way to eliminate our trust in riches is to get rid of them. But notice Paul uses an important phrase: God gives us all we need "for our enjoyment." We can linger on this point and deduce that God gives to us for the purpose of our enjoyment, not for us to simply give away. Live a little! Paul brilliantly continues by affirming indeed we should enjoy using our God-given wealth "to do good."

What if we found joy in being generous to the needy? What if the future we were planning for was a future underprivileged person we believed God would send us to? Fearing the Lord and getting to know His heart, trusting in Jesus for provision in this life and in the age to come, and using wisdom to be ready to participate in ministering a blessing to all you choose to be a neighbor to. That would be *extreme*.

I don't want the blessings of a *balanced* God. My God is extreme. It doesn't cost Him any of His perfect love to dole out perfect discipline. I rejoice in having a True Master who also gave me true freedom (see John 8:36; 1 Peter 2:16). We can't have wisdom without fear of the Lord nor fear of the Lord without a right relationship with God. Yet, a right relationship with God goes hand-in-hand with loving your neighbor as yourself—restoring a right relationship with His image-bearing creatures. Together, these are the welcome sign of the Kingdom of Heaven on earth.

The Parable of the Three Servants has disrupted my life well beyond financial stewardship. Jesus established a family of believers called out to live by His breath. He's entrusted us all with much and expects us to *use well* His resources. We've been given a fortune—our salvation and eternal life, the Gospel and our testimony, a covenant family and the gift of ministry. Our good work is aimed at the least, the last, and the lost. It's not about money. But if we *were* talking about money, that's certainly what we would be talking about.

14

YOUR MONEY'S NO GOOD HERE

The quickest way to get rid of the needy is to meet their needs.

When I started this journey, my plan was to discover the keys to getting out of debt and passionately pursuing my financial goals with the confidence of an unbeatable strategy. I cracked open the Bible app and allowed God to write the formula.

Starting from Genesis, any time something in the Scriptures jumped out at me that sounded like it had to do with finances, I marked it with a green highlight. Somewhere between King David and King Solomon I was blind-sided by the fact that Solomon's story wasn't about manipulating God into making you rich. By the time I got to the words of Jesus, the green highlights seemed to clearly point to what He taught.

Indeed, it is very hard for the rich to enter the Kingdom.

Any time I seek to apply the wisdom of this teaching, I am faced with this reality. It *is* hard. I *want* to use my privilege to benefit those who have less. But I also want the newest iPhone.

I also want a bigger TV. I also want a newer home in a nicer neighborhood ... oh, and with vaulted ceilings. I also want a Tesla. I know these are just luxury items but does it make me a bad person if I still want them?

If, according to Jesus, the Kingdom of God is something within reach today, and that looks like trusting God to meet our needs and then being used by God to meet others' needs with the excess, then maybe so—at the very least, it makes you *feel* like a bad person to look for an alternative to the Kingdom. I must admit, there are days I do not want to participate in this whole Kingdom thing.

Well, guess what? God is not short on options; He always has a remnant. (See Romans 11:2-4.) Throughout the Bible, we see examples of God's people failing to attain the standard set by the Lord and just when you think all hope is lost, God raises up the unexpected to bring a blessing. If I choose not to participate in the Kingdom—same goes for you—I'm sure God will figure something out.

The rich in heaven are those who are not okay with God working out His plan apart from them. This is the most prestigious calling there is. And today, the vision is conceivable. Collectively, the people of God have enough resources to meet every need on the planet. So, what is stopping us?

I believe we know exactly what we need to do but one of two things has us bound: comfort or complacency. Nothing promotes inaction more than **comfort**. When motivated enough to act, nothing stifles the good works of Christ-followers more than **complacency**. We are often blind to this reality because we give in to **comparison**, making ourselves the standard. My pastor says, "comparison causes people to feel prideful or depressed, but never fulfilled." And because it is so easy to see the negative in others, **competition** ensues.

We've got work to do. But to be clear, our solution is not a choice between Legalism and Christendom. The former sees God's grace as a way to become *gooder* while the latter sees God's grace as a way to become *greater*. The truth of Scripture for the second reads like a playbook for an Olympic team—everyone going for the gold in their field. For the first, the truth of Scripture reads like an instruction manual for an Ikea bookshelf—go back and find out what to do with those three extra screws. There are *always* three extra screws.

These camps may seem at odds but they function on the same plane—individuality. By favoring one, we end up interpreting God's heart through our biases and erecting an idea of Him in our own image. Can you imagine what stains the Church could leave if we used His name as an excuse to do what we already wanted? I bet with a simple skim through Church history, you could.

My goal is to make you uncomfortable, not for you to do what you want. I also want you to make your standard Jesus, leaving you unsatisfied by the efforts of man. It is my desire to see you rich in—that is, full of—the Kingdom of Heaven. It is my hope that the whole world would be affected by the expanses of Christ's reign. But make no mistake, the Kingdom of Heaven is not about taking over the world; it's about God's nature taking over you.

Are you full of it? (You saw that one coming.) So, what is getting in the way of you fully participating in the Kingdom of Heaven?

I'll say it—love.

FOR THE MONEY OF LOVE

As a jack of many trades, I get requests every week to use my skills to add value to others. Whether it's as a graphic design artist, printer, DJ, editor, or recording, mixing, and mastering engineer, someone is always asking me to do something they can't do themselves. Skilled labor like this can easily exceed one hundred dollars per hour and that's how most conversations begin: "Are you available on such-and-such date and what's your rate?"

This is where things get complicated. If you've ever had a side hustle, you know that friends and family like getting the "homie hookup" rather than paying what everybody else pays. Everyone likes a deal. This is expected. This is universal. But in the age of social media where everyone has five thousand "friends," what determines who is homie enough to get the hookup?

I know you'd hate to admit it so I'll use myself as an example. The truth is: not everyone gets the same price sheet. As a DJ, I enjoy many different types of music, but I have a love-hate relationship with country music. If at all, I prefer country music the same way I prefer aspirin—as a last resort and in very small doses (and often my headache is worse when it's over). So when I was asked to DJ a four-hour Country Kickback, I was torn between the money I could make and the pure joy it would cost me. When it comes to my craft, I'm no slouch; I always do my homework. In this case, I spent countless hours researching the right songs to play, hoping to find lyrics absent of beer and whiskey. Although my quest to find non-alcoholic country songs wasn't much of a success, the event went off without a hitch and *almost everyone* had a great time—everyone except me. When it was all said and done, I charged my client a hefty premium—double for my trouble.

On the other side of the spectrum, a year prior, I was asked to DJ Chris's wedding. Chris was one of a dozen brothers I made a covenant with in 2012 to do life together, grow together, mourn losses together, and celebrate wins together. Marrying the beautiful, God-fearing woman of his dreams? This was a win. I wasn't sure if he was going to ask me to be his groomsman or his DJ but I already knew as his brother, I was saying yes. He started the conversation as expected: "I was hoping you could DJ the reception. How much will you charge?"

I told him he didn't owe me anything, as long as he was okay with me playing a couple of songs to dance to with my bride, since his two-day wedding eclipsed our date night. When it was all said and done, I gave him and his wife my best and didn't get paid a dime for it.

What's the difference between the former scenario and the latter? There was no difference. Truth be told, both events were longer than a few hours, required a lot of preparation, and included styles of music I wouldn't normally listen to. I wouldn't have taken either of the gigs for the fun of it. I offered both my clients an equal service and I charged them an equal amount.

Sure, I saved Chris thousands but it cost me nothing. How so? I'm glad you asked.

> ## Money is a replacement for love.

In the former gig, my client was a corporation with which I had little to no affiliation. In contrast, I loved my brother Chris and his wife-to-be. Come the end of the night, both clients received an invoice stating the amount of cash it would take to make us even. The newlyweds' account was already settled by our relationship while the first client received a bill.

Money is a replacement for love.

Imagine if you had to rely on your five thousand internet friends for all your basic needs. Who would you count on for food, clothing, and shelter? What about transportation, cell phone, internet, and entertainment? Do any of them love you enough to gift these to you free of charge?

I know someone who used to gift all that to me. Her name is Momma. I've heard a hundred times in my adult years how she used to house me, feed me, and clothe me. She's usually telling me this when I have neglected to return her call for longer than forty-eight hours. *And this is how I repay her!* Of course, these gifts were all her obligation, right? Or were they her honor?

Feeding and cleaning up after someone that can't reciprocate; it's only the close relationship between mother and child that makes it innocuous. Aside from young children and aging parents, most people wouldn't house, feed, dress, and clean up after another person—not for free.

Considering the internet friend scenario, you might be thinking, *Why don't I just get a job?* That's because if you have your own money, you won't need to depend on anyone. When it comes to your friends online, you might be lucky enough to score someone's Netflix password but you can forget about getting the Momma treatment without the Momma relationship.

I can't tell you who built my house, who raised my food, or who made my clothes. Perhaps if I was the previous home-owner's son, I could have been gifted the home. And as much as I feel like besties when I interact with the good folks at Ross, every time I push my cart near the exit they ask, "Are you gonna pay for that?" (I guess there will be no homie hookup today.) And why do the kind people at Chick-fil-A ask for my name and then show me the same prices as the guy in front of me? (I thought we had something special.) But contrary to the impression given by the taste of their chicken, they don't love you like Momma loves you.

Put simply, an economic market is a bunch of people we don't know offering things we can't do or don't want to make ourselves. They hand us their magnum opus and we release our wallets in exchange. So the way we get the things we can't get for ourselves from people with whom we have no relationship is by paying them.

Our payment makes us even.

In the same way, think of how we get the money to pay them. If you don't work in the family business, you likely work for someone you hadn't met or spent any significant amount of time with prior to taking the job. At Quiznos, I recall arduously scrubbing a station full of dishes stacked above my head into the wee hours of the night. My mom, on the other hand, could barely get me to do a sinkful at home, not to mention with any zeal. For the employer, their payment is an attempt to make them even.

To be frank, most people tend to hate their jobs because they feel underpaid—the compensation they receive doesn't make them even.[13] The next big stressor is the people we work alongside. I'm proposing that either way, we're talking about the same thing—relationships. If they paid us well enough we could overlook the lack of relationship; if the relationships we garnered were fruitful, we would focus less on our paychecks. If we had both? Well, that wouldn't be work at all—that would be heaven.

What we also see, and you've done this before, is that monetary gifts help to *avoid* relationships. It's easier to offer that homeless man on the side of the road some pocket change than it is to pull over, have a conversation, and find out what he really needs. Feeding a Lincoln through a thin crack in the window is the less implicating alternative to avoiding eye contact with him as your hand is deep in a bag of hot fries.

In some close relationships, you'd be offended if they attempted to reimburse you financially for your acts of love. Years ago, Kerri and I went on a double date to Chick-fil-A and a movie. Wanting to show how much we loved this couple, we quickly picked up the tab for both, spending about fifty bucks. This means we had to save a couple of months' budget to prepare for this date, so we felt privileged to be able to treat them. When the night was over, they handed us a Christmas card. *Why didn't we think of that!* We opened it to find a hundred dollar bill as a thank you. I don't think I'd ever been more upset at someone giving me money. We've been in low-key competition ever since, trying to out-love one another, and we both feel like we're on the losing end. Jokes on them: as I'm handing out copies of this book to loved ones, guess what's bookmarking this page? My friend, Ben Franklin! (Your move, bro.)

YOU'RE ALL "SET"

You've seen this scene—the guest who is held in high regard insists on paying for his service but the host retorts that his payment isn't necessary. "Your money's no good here." My wife, parents, siblings, nephews, and goddaughters are among those whose payment I wouldn't accept. There isn't an amount of money that can balance out the love I have for them. The answer for them is always *yes*, then I figure out the *how* on my end. In all that I freely give, repayment would send the message, "I want a transaction, not a relationship." For this group, gratitude is a more than sufficient payment. Can you think of some "your money is no good here" relationships in your life?

> "You parents—if your children ask for a loaf of bread, do you give them a stone instead? Or if they

> ask for a fish, do you give them a snake? Of course not! So if you sinful people know how to give good gifts to your children, how much more will your heavenly Father give good gifts to those who ask him." (Matthew 7:9-11)

Now, imagine how The Father must feel when we attempt to circumvent the relationship and repay Him with our good works or by writing a check to the church? With love for God and others at its core, the Kingdom of Heaven should be an economy with no need for money. What belongs to Him belongs to us.

> Since he did not spare even his own Son but gave him up for us all, won't he also give us everything else? (Romans 8:32)

As my pastor puts it: "If God has given us the Big Enchilada, He won't hold back on the chips and salsa!"

Allow me to illustrate my point further. Not too long ago, I was hosting some of my coworkers in my office when we were interrupted by a knock on the door. We paused to find Shy, the wife of another one of my covenant brothers, who worked in the same building. She entered with an urgent request. Speaking in a low tone, as if to keep her words private, she asked, "Can I borrow your car? I need to make a quick run to the bank."

"Here!" I replied as I reached into my desk drawer and handed her the keys. She thanked me quietly as she made a graceful exit.

I tried to regain the momentum of the conversation we were having prior to Shy's interruption but I noticed this whole ordeal left my coworkers confused. I never did work up the nerve to ask them what plagued them but I had an idea.

There's a lot of risk in letting someone borrow your car. We talked about this in Chapter 12, right? Shy was not listed on my insurance policy as one of the named insured, I wasn't going with her, and frankly, I've never actually seen her drive before. Those are just three items on a long list of reasons that handing her the keys would be dumb. All of those things crossed my mind when she asked me and I said yes anyway. I am sure they crossed hers, too. And yet, she asked me anyway.

Only the deepest relationships can cause you to do dumb things on purpose. Who would you let borrow your car? Who would you invite to live in your home rent-free? If that's all small potatoes, to whom would you give your last waffle fry from Chick-fil-A? (Shy had a better chance of getting my car keys than my last waffle fry.) But something she understood, I was just figuring out: those who genuinely love us are incredible resources.

> *As long as we have more than enough, no one we love has to have less than enough.*

While writing this chapter, my wife got news that her job was going to end in the near future. In the meantime, she was still working and our bills were paid. A close friend of ours was between jobs and needed help making ends meet. In this case, he said "bills" (with an S) but didn't specify an amount. Our instinct was to worry about our own future but we chose to trust that the same God who supplied our present excess didn't supply it to make us comfortable. I replied to him, "How much do you need?" On the other side of the phone, I consulted Kerri, "How much can we afford to give?" After praying, we came to this resolution: as long as we have more than enough, no one we love has to have less than enough.

> Now I want you to know, dear brothers and sisters, what God in his kindness has done through the churches in Macedonia. They are being tested by many troubles, and they are very poor. But

> they are also filled with abundant joy, which has
> overflowed in rich generosity.
>
> For I can testify that they gave not only what they
> could afford, but far more. And they did it of their
> own free will. They begged us again and again for
> the privilege of sharing in the gift for the believers in
> Jerusalem. They even did more than we had hoped,
> for their first action was to give themselves to the
> Lord and to us, just as God wanted them to do.
>
> (2 Corinthians 8:1-5)

It was beginning to sound like I was tooting my own horn so
I figured I would let Paul brag on the Macedonian churches for a
brief moment. He says these congregations are not only endur-
ing "many troubles" but they're also "very poor." Nevertheless,
they are rich in generosity, seeing it as their joy and privilege to
give even more than they could afford. Paul's not done:

> You know the generous grace of our Lord Jesus
> Christ. Though he was rich, yet for your sakes he
> became poor, so that by his poverty he could make
> you rich.
>
> Here is my advice: It would be good for you to
> finish what you started a year ago. Last year you
> were the first who wanted to give, and you were the
> first to begin doing it.   (2 Corinthians 8:9-10)

Paul is laying it on thick but don't miss his approach. At first,
he tried to shame—I mean entice—the Corinthian church by
comparing their efforts with those of the poor. He then appeals
to Jesus: if you have anything, if your needs are met, if you
aren't lacking—Jesus made your present state possible through
His sacrificial giving. We owe everything to Jesus but is giving
everything really necessary?

> Whatever you give is acceptable if you give it
> eagerly. And give according to what you have, not
> what you don't have. Of course, I don't mean your
> giving should make life easy for others and hard for
> yourselves. I only mean that there should be some

> equality. Right now you have plenty and can help
> those who are in need. Later, they will have plenty
> and can share with you when you need it. In this
> way, things will be equal.   (2 Corinthians 8:12-14)

Paul touches on a common point of contention with the type of life I'm talking about. It's Airplane Oxygen Mask Theology; I need to take care of myself first and then I'll be in a better position to help others. So, even if I am helping someone else in the process, isn't it unwise to put myself in jeopardy of hardship? The response is simple: if you are ever in need, perhaps they'll be in a position to help you then.

I don't know about you, but after spending several years paying off credit cards, student loans, and the mortgage, and putting money aside to be generous, I reject the thought of ever being in need again. I must admit that this is a hard pill to swallow. My goal is to attain this arbitrary status—"set"—where no matter how much I give, I couldn't go broke if I wanted to. Warren Buffett is set. Bill Gates is set. One day, Chris Mackey will be set.

Here's one more reason the American Dream and the Kingdom Manifesto are incompatible. In the Land of Opportunity, we have the privilege of not having to play the hand we've been dealt. We always have the option to throw in our cards and get a new hand. If we're not satisfied with our current income, we can go back to school and start over in a year or two. If we don't like our skills, neighborhood, religion, or spouse, there's an app that will help find us new ones. The downside of this blessing is we've bought into the belief that we are the author of our destiny, responsible for writing our own story. We have become experts at positioning ourselves for a better shot and greater influence. We think we can glorify God *gooder* if only we were *greater*.

Let's keep it 100. We just don't want to rely on people to meet our needs. Here's the hard truth: being needy does not mean you need people. In the same way, being privileged should stir up an obligation in you but it does not render you responsible to people. We are never poorer than when we presume that God needs our help. God knows the best way because He *is* the Way. People are just a vehicle God chooses to use when *He* blesses the needy.

Take a look at the first verse again. Paul says he's excited to tell what "God ... has done through the churches," not what the churches have done. In verse 5, he explains what was most notable. Not that they gave a bunch of money but "their first action was to give themselves to the Lord," stating it was "just as God wanted them to do."

Whatever you choose to give is adequate (see v. 12) but do you dare ask God for His input or is your mind already made up? Are you dangerous enough to give like this at every opportunity? In addition to looking down on the hard up, we mask our fear by assuming we know what God wants. *God wouldn't want me to give more than I can afford.* If you've ever said what God wouldn't or couldn't do—I know I have—just know, that's where the "city limits" of heaven are set in your life. You are free to give as little or as much as you'd like. You are not rich in heaven based on how much you give away nor are you poor in heaven based on how much you keep. It is the place where you refuse to grant God access that marks the extent of heaven's reign in your life. It's not about emptying your bank account; it's about going to God to see what He would ask of you. That's rich.

In my example, consulting God with my wife was scary. Our friend has a great education, a great network, and great potential to achieve far more than we ever could financially. But what about Kerri's job? What about *our* bills? Well, is God still good? Is God still for us? Then, the rest is above my pay grade. It turned out that the money our friend needed was already set aside in our budget. Our gift didn't send us to the poorhouse. In fact, we all grew richer from the experience.

> You must each decide in your heart how much to give. And don't give reluctantly or in response to pressure. "For God loves a person who gives cheerfully." And God will generously provide all you need. Then you will always have everything you need and plenty left over to share with others. As the Scriptures say, "They share freely and give

> generously to the poor. Their good deeds will be remembered forever." For God is the one who provides seed for the farmer and then bread to eat. In the same way, he will provide and increase your resources and then produce a great harvest of generosity in you.
>
> Yes, you will be enriched in every way so that you can always be generous. And when we take your gifts to those who need them, they will thank God. So two good things will result from this ministry of giving—the needs of the believers in Jerusalem will be met, and they will joyfully express their thanks to God.   (2 Corinthians 9:7-12)

You are rich for a purpose. Give according to the measure of faith God has given you, trusting that He will "generously provide all you need." Paul is unveiling his personal Bible study. First, he suggests Psalm 112 has something to say about you. Then, he alludes to Isaiah 55, which illustrates the benefit of trusting God for our well-being. I encourage you to read these two chapters and get fired up. He concludes that it is a double blessing when God uses us this way—needs are met and God is glorified.

When we're rich in God's love, we can trust Him enough to use us wherever we are. Sometimes I wish God had waited until I was a millionaire before He called me. But we don't have to wait to be "set"—we *are* set! We've got His pocketbook. We're God's beloved kids. We don't have to fear being less than any person but we also won't be free to see ourselves as better than any person. The value of our human counterparts—young, old, poor, rich, male, and female—begins and ends with the Image of God, which we are all collectively made to be.

When we're rich in Kingdom relationships, we get the joy of adding value to the Kingdom by adding (or restoring) value to others. From a perspective of heaven, being greater than our neighbor is not enjoyable—Part B of the Great Commandment entails the very idea that we aren't great until they are great.

When we're rich in humility, we open ourselves up to learn our roles in the family in a clearer way. Read 1 Corinthians 7:17-

24. Paul asserts that God doesn't make mistakes when it comes to who He calls and when. We can imagine a better way but it wouldn't be God's way, which means it wouldn't be *better* at all. He urges believers to remain "as you were," meaning we should make the most of our own status, not seek another's. We ought not expect someone else to pick up the burden of helping our siblings through times of lack when it is within our power to do so. If you truly love those you've chosen a familial relationship with, you're going to have to put your money where your mouth is. Together, there is enough for all to prosper.

Though many, the early believers saw themselves as one. Some people were landowners and homeowners while others had nothing to bring to the table. I'm sure there were all statuses in between. As a whole, they held more than enough resources. Realizing this, they became more blessed by getting rid of all the needy people. How do you eliminate the needy? Meet their needs. Paul used the analogy of the human body and its members to describe our bond. First, he dealt with self-importance, asserting that no member has the right to say they are more important than another. Then he doubles down:

> In fact, some parts of the body that seem weakest and least important are actually the most necessary. And the parts we regard as less honorable are those we clothe with the greatest care. So we carefully protect those parts that should not be seen, while the more honorable parts do not require this special care. So God has put the body together such that extra honor and care are given to those parts that have less dignity. This makes for harmony among the members, so that all the members care for each other. If one part suffers, all the parts suffer with it, and if one part is honored, all the parts are glad.
> (1 Corinthians 12:22-26)

It appears Paul has observed the way Jesus approached Kingdom mathematics. The lowest are given the highest regard. The least and last are given the first priority and greatest care. It's hard to be worried about trivial things when we're tuned into the cries of our own. I think of Major Payne grasping for our pinky finger, asking, "You want me to show you a little trick to get your mind off that pain?" As long as there is suffering in the Body of Christ, there isn't room for selfish concerns.

Paul doesn't end on that downer. Let's not forget that we win as a team. "If one part is honored, all the parts are glad (v. 26)." Any time a member is made to increase, we all have a reason to celebrate. If individualism is off the table, we have a better chance at fulfilling our commission.

In the final chapter, we're going to discuss what that commission looks like in light of all we've learned.

15

NO LIMIT

Consider this the book's bonus track.

The question I always get when discussing this idea of becoming rich in heaven is: *How far should I take this?* This is all good in theory, but in the real world, we've got valid excuses. As great as my examples were in Chapter 14, we all know that you can't trust strangers, we're way too busy, and we don't make enough money to help everyone we meet. Jesus is our example.

The ministry of Jesus began with the message, "The Kingdom of Heaven is near" (see Matthew 4:17). This is how Jesus chose to reveal the heart of the Father: He came near even to us before we trusted Him (see Romans 5:6-8). As I mentioned earlier, God's love is the welcome sign letting you know heaven is here. Welcome signs serve several purposes: populace, disposition, economy, and boundaries, to name a few. We have discussed the gamut of the Kingdom of Heaven, learning how Jesus is its model citizen (He's also the King) and His teachings detail the character of those who announce its arrival. Last chapter, we talked about its economics and its "city limits," identifying where the jurisdiction of its power begins and ends.

You have been called and chosen by God to participate in His Great Kingdom (1 Peter 2:9). This is not because you have done anything good nor because you are inherently good, but because of the goodness that exists solely in Him (Deuteronomy 9:6; Titus 3:5). By your membership in the Kingdom, you have access to the vaults of Heaven to accomplish anything that aligns with the will of the King (Philippians 4:19). Although nothing is required of you to gain access to God's Kingdom, you will respond according to how much your heart has internalized the magnitude of the gift you've been given (Luke 7:41-43). Your response is linked to your heavenly bank account (Matthew 19:21). The greater your response, the more it will require you to trust in Him. You can have as much of the riches of the Kingdom as you want. You can have as little of the Kingdom as you want. The Kingdom of Heaven is wherever you choose to invite Jesus.

Jesus is the boundary line.

Jesus is the demographic.

Jesus is the currency.

The most extreme thing you can do in the Kingdom isn't selling all your possessions and giving it to the poor; it's trusting God enough to let Him set the boundary in your life. For some, that may mean giving 100 percent for a season; for others, it could mean being on the receiving end for a season and giving zero. If you just thought *no way* to either of those without first hearing from God, then that is where you have drawn the boundary. I can't tell you what to give, how much, and when. I can't tell you what influence God should have in your decision-making process. It's not that easy. It's going to look different for you than it will for me.

Realize I'm talking about doing the impossible here. In Mark 10:26, the disciples essentially ask Jesus, "If the rich can't get to heaven, then who in the world can be saved?"

> Jesus looked at them intently and said, "Humanly speaking, it is impossible. But not with God. Everything is possible with God."   (Mark 10:27)

There isn't a formula for passing a camel through the eye of a needle, and it would be just as foolish to try to whip up a one-size-fits-all prescription for *this* impossible task. But since Jesus summed it up in two words ("with God"), I can sum it up in one—Jesus. He is our Immanuel, or "God with us" (see Isaiah 7:14). We are going to express our faithfulness to God differently, but if we heed the words of Jesus, we will all be doing the same thing: trusting Him.

So, how far should you take this? Well, how far did Jesus take it?

WHAT SHOULD WE DO?

This is where the rubber meets the road in all we've learned. Our Master has gone away on a temporary trip and He's entrusted to us everything we call our own—our money, our education, our careers, our time, our motivation, our relationships. He wants us to use all these resources well.

If we continue reading in Matthew 25, Jesus paints us one final portrait, comparing the Final Judgment to that awkward moment in PE class where everyone is split into two teams. Actually, He says it's more like a shepherd separating sheep from goats. He puts the ones who are righteous on His right side and the ones who are left ... go to His left. Make sense? Then, King Jesus tells the righteous ones they won the grand and glorious jackpot (yes, that was a *Willy Wonka* reference). He explains the reasoning behind their acceptance: they took care of Him when He was in need.

> "Then these righteous ones will reply, 'Lord, when did we ever see you hungry and feed you? Or thirsty and give you something to drink? Or a stranger and show you hospitality? Or naked and give you clothing? When did we ever see you sick or in prison and visit you?'
> "And the King will say, 'I tell you the truth, when you did it to one of the least of these my

> brothers and sisters, you were doing it to me!'"
>
> (Matthew 25:37-40)

We've already talked about what it looks like to bless those in need, but what I love most about this account is the response of the righteous ones. These folks weren't trying to get to heaven by handing out water bottles, and they were pleasantly surprised to hear their report card. It doesn't appear they realized what their deeds meant to the King.

From Matthew 25 and its given context, it is apparent that Jesus wants our relationship with Him to affect every other relationship we are allowed. It's one thing to see those who love you as incredible resources, but it's an even greater blessing when you see your life as a resource for those you will love. Imagine what resources could flow through you if you genuinely loved people more. Instead of seeing our actions as loving people "for God," we can learn to just love people. When we get it right, we won't even realize we're doing it.

When it comes to separating people, I don't do it quite like Jesus. I don't know about you, but I like to keep my relationships in neat categories—my friends, my family; they have separate roles and I prefer them in separate houses. My coworkers belong in the office, and there's nothing worse than running into a "stray" at the grocery store. *Oh, you buy food, too? Well, one of us isn't supposed to be here.*

We make categories for our neighbors, clients, service workers, business partners, students, bosses, coaches, mentors, siblings, blood family, extended family, church family—the list goes on. Any way we choose to slice it, we're given the same order of business from our Headquarters: agape (or "love").

Agape is the key to transcending the individualism celebrated by the world we live in because *agape* is a mindset borne of selflessness, self-denial, and to a certain degree, self-forgetfulness. It is a matter of desiring to see goodness wherever you go and imparting it where you see it lacking. As I reflect on 1 Corinthians 13, which was read before God and witnesses at my wedding, I recall that we weren't just given this description of God's love to model for our spouses but we were also instructed to take on this attitude when dealing with those who are hostile toward us (see Matthew 5:43-44). This was demonstrated by God through Christ, who loved even those who were hostile toward Him.

Following the resurrection of Jesus, those early followers and apostolic leaders—a diverse group of men and women spanning various social classes, backgrounds, and traditions—had the task of walking out everything they said they believed. These events, recorded in the Book of Acts, illustrate what the rich in heaven look like in real life. See what happens when Peter makes an appeal to one large group during a holy day meeting.

> Peter's words pierced their hearts, and they said to him and to the other apostles, "Brothers, what should we do?"
>
> Peter replied, "Each of you must repent of your sins and turn to God, and be baptized in the name of Jesus Christ for the forgiveness of your sins. Then you will receive the gift of the Holy Spirit. This promise is to you, to your children, and to those far away —all who have been called by the Lord our God." Then Peter continued preaching for a long time, strongly urging all his listeners, "Save yourselves from this crooked generation!"
>
> Those who believed what Peter said were baptized and added to the church that day—about 3,000 in all.   (Acts of the Apostles 2:37-41)

First, the Apostle Peter gave them the practical walkthrough on how to become a follower of Jesus. Then it says he kept preaching for them to get out of the system because it's all going down. I'm guessing he read to them the last few chapters of this book but that's only speculation. Here's what the emergence looked like for the early Church:

> All the believers devoted themselves to the apostles' teaching, and to fellowship, and to sharing in meals (including the Lord's Supper), and to prayer. A deep sense of awe came over them all,

> and the apostles performed many miraculous signs
> and wonders. And all the believers met together
> in one place and shared everything they had.
> (Acts of the Apostles 2:42-44)

You can see the response was uniform. They were all committed to the teaching, the fellowship, the breaking of bread, and the prayer together. Their identity was grounded in *koinonia*, not individualism. *Koinonia* is the Greek word translated "fellowship" and carries with it the idea of partners who share in the rewards.

> They sold their property and possessions and
> shared the money with those in need. They
> worshiped together at the Temple each day, met
> in homes for the Lord's Supper, and shared their
> meals with great joy and generosity — all the
> while praising God and enjoying the goodwill of
> all the people. And each day the Lord added to
> their fellowship those who were being saved.
> (Acts of the Apostles 2:45-47)

It doesn't say whether or not Peter instructed them to respond this way, but it does give a hint. Remember our discussion on fear of the Lord? We see in verse 42, a "deep sense of awe came over them all" which is most certainly the reverential fear that makes ten-talent servants. I don't want to read too much into the literal order of this description, but it doesn't say that the believers were in awe of the miraculous signs. Sure, that would do it, too, but just imagine: if you saw thousands of strangers from different backgrounds all getting along and treating each other like family, wouldn't you be in awe? It seems they valued the association and participation with the goodness and greatness of God more than they valued making themselves *gooder* or *greater*. It is this type of God-fearing culture that makes a community ripe for seeing a regular occurrence of miracles, signs, and wonders in their midst.

BEYOND BELIEF

Further, let's talk about the miraculous for a moment. Where does your mind go when you hear the phrase "signs and wonders"? If you're like me, you think of hilarious videos of Benny Hinn knocking a crowd off their feet with one wave. If you're less cynical, perhaps you recall a powerful testimony of cancer being healed or back pain relieved. As you continue reading through the Book of Acts, you'll see what is meant. Yes, the lame walk, demons flee, the dead rise—yet most of the wonders aren't spoken of in that specific language. Between Peter's sermon in Chapter 2 and Paul's conversion in Chapter 9, the only clear signs we read about that would qualify in our modern charismatic movement are the healing of the lame man (see Acts 3) and the laying on of hands to receive the Holy Spirit (see Acts 8:17).

What we *do* see in between are things we often don't associate with the wonders of God. We see the supernatural intervention of God defending the fruitful multiplication of His holy people. The power of the Spirit at work arrives in quakes and also brings a couple to an untimely death. We also see the boldness to preach the Good News of Jesus and the rapid expansion of true believers. Let's just call the former what it is: scary. The latter isn't very marketable in today's culture, either. Since we've boiled down salvation to raising your hand with your head bowed and eyes closed while whispering a prayer over smooth jazz, we discount solid preaching and we forget how miraculous the gift of belief is and how fond of it God is. In Luke 15, as Jesus shares parables about the lost being found, He says, "In the same way, there is more joy in heaven over one lost sinner who repents and returns to God than over ninety-nine others who are righteous and haven't strayed away!" (Luke 15:7). You'll see that the Book of Acts is careful to mention repentance, salvation, community, and faith following every account of miraculous signs and wonders. But does the idea of believers believing leave us in awe?

"Not everyone who calls out to me, 'Lord! Lord!'

> will enter the Kingdom of Heaven. Only those who
> actually do the will of my Father in heaven will
> enter. On judgment day many will say to me, 'Lord!
> Lord! We prophesied in your name and cast out
> demons in your name and performed many miracles
> in your name.' But I will reply, 'I never knew you.
> Get away from me, you who break God's laws.'"
>
> (Matthew 7:21-23)

If we pay close attention to the words spoken by Jesus, we can't simply be satisfied by prophecy, deliverance, or any other miracles we see. For the Kingdom of Heaven, the rites of passage seem to be something more than miracles, signs, and wonders. More valuable, like doing the Father's will.

> "And this is the will of him who sent me, that I
> should lose nothing of all that he has given me, but
> raise it up on the last day. For this is the will of my
> Father, that everyone who looks on the Son and
> believes in him should have eternal life, and I will
> raise him up on the last day."   (John 6:39-40 ESV)

The will of God begins with a two-step process: (1) look at Jesus; (2) trust in Him. The ongoing wonder of all the history of Christianity is a divine trust in the work of Jesus. Are you trusting in Christ alone that your eternal status is settled? That is the will of the Father. We can't afford to miss the significance of belief and where it comes from. Showing your work in the Kingdom starts with trusting our lives with Him.

> "No one can come to me unless the Father who
> sent me draws him. And I will raise him up on the
> last day."   (John 6:44 ESV)

Don't forget that this is the Lord's doing. Paul takes this idea a step further:

> For by grace you have been saved through faith.
> And this is not your own doing; it is the gift of God,
> not a result of works, so that no one may boast. For

> we are his workmanship, created in Christ Jesus for
> good works, which God prepared beforehand, that
> we should walk in them.   (Ephesians 2:8-10 ESV)

Your faith is a precious gift God has given to you. Notice how it isn't given because *of* good works, but it is given *for* good works. Trusting in Christ isn't the end of the process, but having faith is a miracle. If we truly believed this, perhaps we would take getting to know Jesus more seriously.

> No one who abides in him keeps on sinning; no
> one who keeps on sinning has either seen him or
> known him.   (1 John 3:6 ESV)

Our lives will not automatically look different as a result of believing in Jesus. You will bear fruit only to the degree which you respond to His gift. If we read the above passage without considering the previous ones, we could conclude our Christian duty is to stop sinning. It's not. We need to see Him (as in John 6) and know Him, or (as in Matthew 7) be known by Him. We can see this is accomplished by abiding (or making our home base) in Jesus. Sin is simply evidence of our residence.

Sin means to fail or "miss the mark." Sure, I could start listing the million-and-one ways people can miss the mark, or I can remind you of the target. Remember, Jesus answered the "most important" question by saying our goal is to love Him and others. When we fail at *agape*, we break His law. When we fully grasp the incredible goodness of the gift of belief, it ought to result in a great love for others. This is what it means to know Him.

> Anyone who does not love does not know God,
> because God is love.   (1 John 4:8 ESV)

I've made my point. Seeing Jesus is a great miracle; trusting in Him, even more. Making our home in Him is a great sign; loving others, an awesome wonder. Now, in light of the truth of eternity and the present age we're living in, what is the most loving thing we can do? As a believer, you have the simple task of doing the will of the Father which was done for you: showing others Jesus. Are you allowing the people who cross your path to look on Jesus that they may believe in Him?

> But how can they call on him to save them unless they believe in him? And how can they believe in him if they have never heard about him? And how can they hear about him unless someone tells them?
> (Romans 10:14)

I'm not asking anything of you that Jesus hasn't already done Himself. Jesus said about His ministry, "He does only what he sees the Father doing" (John 5:19). Later in an exchange with His band of misfits, He has to break it down for them plainly:

> "If you had really known me, you would know who my Father is. From now on, you do know him and have seen him!"
> Philip said, "Lord, show us the Father, and we will be satisfied."
> Jesus replied, "Have I been with you all this time, Philip, and yet you still don't know who I am? Anyone who has seen me has seen the Father! So why are you asking me to show him to you? Don't you believe that I am in the Father and the Father is in me? The words I speak are not my own, but my Father who lives in me does his work through me."
> (John 14:7-10)

Christ Jesus sets the standard for Christlikeness. Yet in His ministry, He attributed both His words and His deeds to the Father. He prays, "I have revealed you to them, and I will continue to do so. Then your love for me will be in them, and I will be in them" (John 17:26). This was His mission and we will do well to make it ours. If you get to know Jesus, His Holy Spirit will work miracles in and through you, and people who get to know you will hear about Him and see Him.

When we speak of these things with boldness, we also give evidence of the Spirit at work. In a world where only extreme messaging gets attention, boldness is overlooked and undervalued. In Acts 4, Peter and John are left to defend their act of healing before the council and they addressed them while "filled with the Holy Spirit" (see Acts 4:8). Check out the council's response.

> The members of the council were amazed when they saw the boldness of Peter and John, for they could see that they were ordinary men with no special training in the Scriptures. They also recognized them as men who had been with Jesus. But since they could see the man who had been healed standing right there among them, there was nothing the council could say.
>
> (Acts of the Apostles 4:13-14)

The Holy Spirit makes ordinary people extraordinary. These religious folk seemed to be more astonished at Peter's and John's boldness than the healing of a lifelong ailment. If you recall, the forty-year-old man who had been unable to walk from birth was begging beside the gate of the Temple before they pulled him to his feet. All he was asking for was a little money. Can you imagine if Peter or John simply carried pocket change? Perhaps he would have died lame, or worse, died without Christ.

Can people tell you've been with Jesus? Are you surrounding yourself with Spirit-filled believers making much of Jesus and little of themselves? The rich in heaven are ordinary people living in love, joy, peace, patience, kindness, goodness, faithfulness, gentleness, and self-control. (see Galatians 5:22-23).

> ## *The Holy Spirit makes ordinary people extraordinary.*

The apostles were reprimanded that day as the council "commanded them never again to speak or teach in the name of Jesus" (see Acts 4:18). Once they were let go, they returned to the fellowship of believers who sent up a unified prayer to be filled with the same boldness that Peter and John were given so they could break the rules together. This is *koinonia* at work.

> And now, O Lord, hear their threats, and give us, your servants, great boldness in preaching your word.   (Acts of the Apostles 4:29)

We must dive deeper here. Following these events, we are given a description that is reminiscent of Acts 2:42-47.

> After this prayer, the meeting place shook, and they were all filled with the Holy Spirit. Then they preached the word of God with boldness.
> All the believers were united in heart and mind. And they felt that what they owned was not their own, so they shared everything they had. The apostles testified powerfully to the resurrection of the Lord Jesus, and God's great blessing was upon them all. There were no needy people among them, because those who owned land or houses would sell them and bring the money to the apostles to give to those in need. (Acts of the Apostles 4:31-35)

We are coming off the heels of some of the greatest miracles we have ever seen. It started with one man resurrected and now we have seen thousands resurrected to new life. Everyone is in loving communion with one another and sharing all they have. The richest among them gave up their means to benefit those with the greatest need. This sounds a lot like socialism, but recognize that no government body forced this redistribution of wealth. This was a welfare program proposed by the unity of heart in the Church and enacted through the power of the Holy Spirit.

You want to know why we don't see more Acts 2 and 4 Christians? Because we don't see Acts 2 and 4 Christians. The rich in heaven are hard to find. The heart of God, however, is infectious; the more you see it in action, the more you'll want to be a part of it. Wherever heaven shows up, God's wonder spreads like wildfire. We call this revival. Conversely, wherever the cares of the world eclipse heaven, apathy spreads like the plague. We call this Monday.

Let's not forget how it all started. This act of the Holy Spirit began with believers *not* giving any money. Instead, they were able to meet a need greater than money by the power of Christ within them. That's what happens when all you have to your name is the name of Jesus. That's rich.

Later in Acts, Paul acknowledges what he truly values in his life and where his riches come from.

> "But my life is worth nothing to me unless
> I use it for finishing the work assigned me by
> the Lord Jesus—the work of telling others the
> Good News about the wonderful grace of God."
> (Acts of the Apostles 20:24)

The first and greatest miracle we have at our fingertips is our faith. If we have it, our trust in the Good News is something we are always free to give to others. If we have it, it's something that doesn't need clarification or a confirmation. We are encouraged, "if someone asks about your hope as a believer, always be ready to explain it" (see 1 Peter 3:15). Paul also says the Good News about Christ "is the power of God at work, saving everyone who believes" (see Romans 1:16). Today, billions more have experienced the miracle of faith and reconciliation to the Father.[14] Don't forget the miracle He has done in you and you'll carry the miraculous wherever you go.

Can you say your life would be "worth nothing" if you kept Jesus to yourself? Here is the sad reality: if you decide to abort the mission now, you can still find a way to make your life "worth something" apart from Jesus. But you're already rich in this world. Does being richer reflect what you truly value? If so, I can promise you that you'll experience less of the Kingdom as a result. I won't go so far as to say your salvation depends on it—but someone else's might.

The rich in heaven consider their "worth" worthless if Christ isn't the focus. Being Christocentric gives everything you do a voice to preach His Good News. Heaven is wherever God has access. So, make His residence your residence. When you dwell in Him, He will dwell in you and you will be able to do what you see Him doing. Not only that, Jesus says, "I tell you the truth, anyone who believes in me will do the same works I have done, and even greater works, because I am going to be with the Father" (John 14:12). You will see more of what He does and how He operates when you delve into the Word with a like-minded friend and look for Him in His Word. The rich in heaven are rich in His Word. The rich in heaven are rich in *koinonia*. The rich in heaven are rich in *agape*.

Your life is more than a Bible study; it's an open-book test. So don't be afraid to do life with the Good Book open. I hope that by accentuating key words and phrases and highlighting themes that permeate Scripture, I have kindled your desire to show your work. In this case, show "the work assigned to you by the Lord." In my experience, I have found the best first step to a Christ-centered perspective is reading the Word. Instead of reading the Bible in light of your priorities, will you now read your priorities in light of the Bible?

We started this journey by examining our motivators and taking an inventory of what we value. The effectiveness of this book will be measured in direct proportion to your amenability in this area. You may decide to revisit your Why List and Why Not List if you've had a "life" or "death" experience during this season—that is, if something you've read has made a lasting impact. It may be time to revive some dreams you've written off, or perhaps it's time to bury the false priorities which keep popping up. No matter which path you choose, there is no limit. The only question is how you prefer your riches—on earth or in heaven?

> "But many who are the greatest now will
> be least important then, and those who seem
> least important now will be the greatest then."
> (Mark 10:31)

ENDNOTES

1   Catherine Rampell, "The Haves and the Have-Nots," *New York Times*, January 31, 2011, https://economix.blogs. nytimes.com/2011/01/31/the-haves-and-the-have-nots/.

2   Eric Rosenbaum, "Millions of Americans are only $400 away from financial hardship. Here's why," *CNBC*, May 23, 2019, https://www.cnbc.com/2019/05/23/millions-of-americans-are-only-400-away-from-financial-hardship.html.

3   Hyrum W. Smith, *The 10 Natural Laws of Successful Time and Life Management* (New York: Warner Books, 1994), 48.

4   "Model S Specs," *Tesla*, Palo Alto, CA (April 2019), https://www. tesla.com/models.

5   Chris Prentice, "Americans are drinking a daily cup of coffee at the highest level in six years: survey," *Reuters*, March 17, 2018, https://www.reuters.com/article/us-coffee-conference-survey/americans-are-drinking-a-daily-cup-of-coffee-at-the-highest-level-in-six-years-survey-idUSKCN1GT0KU.

6   Jessica Semega, et al., "Income and Poverty in the United States: 2018," *U.S. Census Bureau*, P60-266 (September 2019): 1, https://www.census.gov/library/publications/2019/demo/p60-266.html.

7   McLeod Brown & Chris Kolmar, "An Interactive Exploration Of Dead End Careers," *Zippia*, July 10, 2018, https://www. zippia.com/research/dead-end-careers/.

8   Liu Yi Lin et al., "Association Between Social Media Use And Depression Among U.S. Young Adults," *Depression and Anxiety 33*, no. 4 (April 1, 2016): 323–31, https://doi.org/10.1002/da.22466.

9   Katherine Hobson, "Feeling Lonely? Too Much Time On Social Media May Be Why," *NPR*, March 6, 2017, https://www.npr.org/sections/health-shots/2017/03/06/518362255/.

10 Howard Dayton, *Your Money Counts* (Carol Stream, IL: Tyndale House Publishers, 2011), 2.

11 Dave Ramsey, *The Total Money Makeover* (Nashville, TN: Thomas Nelson, 2003), 125.

12 A. W. Tozer, *The Knowledge of the Holy* (Zeeland, MI: Reformed

Church Publications, 2017), 76.

13 "Accounting Principals & Ajilon Research & Insights,"
Accounting Principals, Jacksonville, FL (May 2018), https://www.
accountingprincipals.com/~/media/AdeccoGroup/Brands/
AccountingPrincipals%20Brand/USA/media/downloads/FO_Big%20
Rock%20Deck_May%202018.pdf.

14 "The Changing Global Religious Landscape," *Pew Research
Center*, Washington, D.C. (April 2017), https://www.
pewforum.org/2017/04/05/the-changing-global-religious-landscape/.

ACKNOWLEDGEMENTS

First giving honor to God, who is the head of my life. To my pastor, first lady, all the ministers, deacons, mothers, missionaries, saints, and friends ... All jokes aside, I can't let anything testify of the goodness and greatness of the Lord on my behalf. I thank the Lord that He guided me to the right church, right when I needed it. He held my hand during this process, gave me grace to write what He told me to, and didn't take that privilege away when I failed to *use well*. If Yeshua goes with me, I won't stop writing about His riches.

Kerri, thank you for being my *ezer* throughout our journey. Your steadfast love for Jesus (even more than your love for me) will continue to inspire me to heaven and beyond. I'm rich because you're so rich. I love you.

Wayne & Shequan, thank you for diving in the Word with us all these years and being a sounding board for these crazy ideas I've worked out. To see how we've grown richer in Christ together means everything.

Parental units, you've blessed me with the most valuable asset I possess—my faith. Thank you for the sacrifices you made to keep me close to Jesus.

Chad, thank you for discipling me and lighting the spark which got this whole brushfire going. You made the initial investment into my faith journey; your faithfulness is paying dividends. I pray you see that your labor was not in vain.

If not for Elevate International, I never would have accidentally written the outline for this book. So to my Elevate family, thanks for demonstrating true servant leadership and drawing things out of me that I didn't even know were in me.

Troy & Ashley, thank you for showing me what Rich in Heaven looked like before I had the words.

Cory & Amy, thank you for teaching the words. You have a knack for practical theology, but most of all, you walk the talk.

Ivan, I'd still be writing right now if not for you. Thank you for pushing me to the finish line. Actually, just one more edit ...